Binge <small>and</small> Sprint

From Endless Cake
To Recovery

NAOMI JOSEPH

North Carolina

Published in the United States by WriteLife Publishing
(an imprint of Boutique of Quality Books Publishing Company)
www.writelife.com

978-1-60808-265-0 (p)
978-1-60808-266-7 (e)

Library of Congress Control Number: 2021947837

Book Design by Robin Krauss, www.bookformatters.com
Cover Design by Rebecca Lown, www.rebeccalowndesign.com
First editor: Andrea Vande Vorde
Second editor: Allison Itterly

Praise for Binge and Sprint and Naomi Joseph

"Readers will find Naomi's journey about her battle with food, and compulsive worker-bee behavior to be emotionally profound and engrossing. It is a page turner as Naomi addresses you "dear reader" you are drawn into her struggles with a "dark voice" in her head, that she is not good enough! It is chock full of Jewish witticisms and quotes from the Torah.

As an eating disorders expert and the long term moderator of a highly sophisticated book club in the Five Towns, I find Naomi's story to be raw, riveting and poignant! It leaves the reader with tools for recovery to a place of understanding and acceptance. A must read!"

> — Dr. Ellen Schor Haimoff, Ph.D., clinical Psychologist,
> Director of the Associates for Bulemia and Related
> Disorders in Manhattan, author of introduction to
> *Why are they Starving Themselves?* by Elaine Landau

———————————

"An honest and powerful story, Naomi takes us on a journey of her challenges to give us the strength to overcome ours."

> — Charlie Harary, investor, strategic adviser, professor,
> motivational speaker, radio show host, television
> personality and author of *Unlocking Greatness:
> The Unexpected Journey from the Life you Have
> to the Life You Want*

———————————

"In this book, Naomi Joseph explores the roots of her lifelong struggle with binge eating with unflinching honesty and humor. She puts a magnifying glass on how the most painful aspects of her life influenced her relationship with herself and by extension, with food. Weaving in her experience of growing up in a religious Jewish community, we see how food provided solace yet also created heart-wrenching conflict. Regardless of religion or culture, all readers who struggle with food will relate to the "Dark Voice" within, the voice of shame, the voice that tells us we aren't good enough. Similarly resonant is the image of an ideal self she calls "Summer," which highlights the cultural trap of perfectionism and how it impacts us. Realizing that bingeing is a way of coping with the exigencies of life, she explores new ways of being and relating with the world, all of which changes the way she eats. At its heart, B*inge and Sprint* is the story of psychological birth, which is messy, painful, funny, and ultimately hopeful."

> — Dr. Nina Savelle-Rocklin, PsyD, radio show host and
> author of *Food for Thought: Perspectives on Eating
> Disorders* and *The Binge Cure: 7 Steps to Outsmart
> Emotional Eating*

"Naomi has created a compelling narrative that incorporates humor, honesty, and self-reflection. Her approach to storytelling takes a serious challenge that many people hide in shame and brings it to light in a way that makes it totally relatable. I read this book in two days and felt like I was indulging in a novel. Naomi has written a triumph that humanizes the way those in conflict with food view themselves, and will help their loved ones and support system better understand their dance with food."

> — Kim MacGregor, Wellness Entrepreneur,
> Transformation coach, Author, Speaker

Table of Contents

"The search for the beloved
is fulfilled when
you fall in love with yourself."

—Alan Cohen

Foreword

By Ira M. Sacker, MD
Eating Disorders Specialist
Author of *Dying to Be Thin* and *Regaining Your Self*

I meet each patient with an initial assessment without knowing their life journey ahead of time. So, gathering personal and family history is extremely pertinent to shape the picture of where the patient presently is with an eating disorder. Everyone is different. They can start therapy a few months or several years after the initial behaviors start. Some sample what therapy is by trying out a therapy session(s) but cannot find a therapist they can connect to. Then there are others who have been drowning for decades with disordered eating. Finally, there are some who believe they are the only ones going through this, so they live in silence.

Patients reach out for help either independently or because of someone else. I am proud of all my patients who accept help and take the risk to change. I have been allowed to witness their successes beyond recovery. Finishing high school, travel, graduation from university, dating, marriage, pregnancy, having a family, setting up a home, professional career, and attaining life goals are just some of the examples.

I have been treating eating disorders for over forty-five years. I graduated from UCLA School of Medicine. After my residency at NYU, I was fortunately not drafted for Vietnam and instead got stationed in Frankfurt, Germany, to establish the Frankfurt Youth Health Center. After three years in Europe, I was relocated back to New York where I became Chief of Adolescence Medicine at Brookdale University Hospital in Brooklyn, New York. I started my private practice on Long Island in the 1980s and expanded to Manhattan when I retired from Brookdale in 2005.

My work in Brooklyn made connections with influential rabbis, and that granted me an opportunity to work with many Orthodox communities. I was raised in an Orthodox home. My Bubbe (grandmother) from Russia only spoke Yiddish. She lived with us during my formative years, and that was how I learned Yiddish expressions and context. Both sets of grandparents came to America by 1900, so none of my family was directly affected by the Holocaust. However, my wife's maternal family almost lost everyone. Her parents left Budapest, Hungary, in October 1938, eleven months before World War II started. They sponsored a nephew to come to New York. He was the only remaining family member who survived the death camps. My in-laws and their nephew shared all the devastating stories of World War II and the Holocaust. This has impacted me forever.

My desire to help the generations of individuals who survived the Holocaust grew from here. I was not sure what it would look like. As a specialist in eating disorders, I have treated many generations of Holocaust survivors, their children, their grandchildren, and their great-grandchildren.

DNA imprint from trauma experienced in the Holocaust has been suspected to have an increased risk of eating disorders for the following generations. The development of an eating disorder in the Jewish community is prevalent. So much so that it falls into a hidden, secret category due to the effect on marriage and fertility issues. There are also limitations for seeking treatment.

Naomi came to see me through a referral from the Orthodox community. While discussing her family history, I learned that she had family members who were Holocaust survivors, her grandparents emigrated from Europe, and her parents were First Generation American.

Once in recovery from binge eating, Naomi had a desire to write a book. Her passion for wanting to help others is why she put pen to paper. We both were similar in wanting to help the individuals who are still struggling and remain voiceless. This is a powerful memoir of her life journey with a reoccurring message: You are not alone, and there is always hope.

In the Beginning

My observations of Naomi, aside from her being extremely task-oriented, was that she overworked herself, and she could never figure out when she would be the priority. Taking a pause was completely impossible because goals had to be met in every aspect of her life from her marriage, children, family, friends, and especially in her work life. A frequent response to a suggestion for putting herself first was, "I don't have time for that." Naomi is not alone; I see this difficulty to grasp the notion of self-care constantly.

New Concept

Naomi's reason for therapy was wanting change that lasted. First, I have to teach the basics of how an eating disorder functions. Any form of an eating disorder is never solely about the food. Binge eating is a symptom, not the underlying issue. It's not about discovering that fabulous diet, the perfect food plan, or success at the latest trends. None of these will stop binge eating. There needs to be a realization that there is an association between food and feelings. By not connecting to the feelings, food behaviors originate and hide core issues. Examples of underlying core issues are self-doubt, shame, guilt, never feeling good enough, comparisons to others, depression, anxiety, trauma, lack of control, and being voiceless.

Breakthrough

In order to face these core issues, an awareness needs to take place when justifying or escaping to bingeing begins. The trigger response of large quantities of food to mouth never really fills a void. Accept that binge eating is happening. Then stop and look at the patterns that break down the hidden reasons for why it is occurring. Be aware that this will unearth feelings instead of filling the empty void. Beneath that discovery of feelings associated to core issues is when the healing begins. Finding a balance between the mind and body is key.

Recovery

I believe any individual can completely recover from an eating disorder. This comes from an understanding that we have limitations, we are not perfect, and we need to give ourselves permission to be human along with acceptance, forgiveness, gratitude, and the gift of bravery.

Introduction

For my entire life, I identified as fat or skinny. I had two moods when it came to my weight: positively happy or completely miserable. Either I was doing fabulously or I was on the couch unable to function, dying on the inside from both food and emotional overload. Over the last four decades, I swung wildly like Maimonides's pendulum, from one end of the spectrum to the other, when it came to my eating habits. After forty years of suffering, I was finally able to find middle ground and begin to attain recovery from binge eating, that place of achieving a balanced state where I am in alignment with my soul and who I am supposed to be.

My unhealthy relationship with food began when I was eight years old. This war with food lasted for over forty years. Binge eating, mindless eating, pigging out, stuffing your face, snack-attack, snackccident, compulsive overeating, emotional eating, foodie, abusing food, food connoisseur . . . whatever you call it, on a practical level it all results in the same thing: a lifelong war with food. Food, the very gift that was meant to nourish you to your best self, instead gets distorted in endless ways.

I never planned to be at war with food or myself for that matter. Sure, we could blame history, upbringing, family traditions, or heredity in our DNA. Truly, I take responsibility for creating my own prison. I didn't mean to invite binge eating into my life. I certainly wouldn't have knowingly chosen this particular life challenge. One where I have jammed unthinkable quantities of food down my throat, been disgusted with myself for doing it, and then just prayed that it would all magically go away, knowing all along that the whole process would just start over again.

For almost my entire life, I've been heavily steeped in the war with food, and now I am not. If your heart is yearning for the same thing, then please join me on my journey so that you, too, can learn the lessons that have brought me to recovery. If you've had a consistent, never-ending battle with food, know that I have endured with you. My journey through binge eating has brought me to my knees and destroyed my self-worth a thousand times. But I will tell you that binge eating has been one of my greatest teachers, and I wouldn't have traded my journey for anything in the world because it's made me who I am today.

The long and arduous process to recovery has taught me how to feed my life's purpose instead of listening to the dark voices in my head. I've learned how to release what I perceived as the unworthy parts of me, and with it, the exhaustion from carrying those struggles that were never even mine to hold. This evolution brought forth perseverance, love, understanding, empathy, kindness, gratitude, grit, and integrity. You don't have to obey the dark voice in your head because it is consistently and negatively driving you to destroy your sense of self. Yes, you'll fall down. But then you get to pick yourself back up, and therein lies your golden opportunities for growth.

After a lifetime of getting knocked to the ground by the same opponent and then rising repeatedly, you get to know the dark voice's game pretty well. You begin to understand the strategies it employs, the buttons it pushes, and the mind games it holds over you. Once you can slowly turn up the volume and really listen to exactly what that dark voice has been saying, you can understand it and beat it at its own game. You'll recognize your weak spots and learn how to strengthen them, and then you can use those weaknesses as an ironclad shield against its tricks. And then you'll rise to the next level, which introduces improvement of your physical self through strength, your mental self through wisdom, and your spiritual self through G-d's gifts in epic proportions.

It is in this space that you will give yourself grace when things don't go as planned. You will decide to eat one or two cookies for a little joy without throwing in the towel and consuming the entire box. You will know you look fabulous no matter what you weigh. You will feel justified in rewarding yourself for the small hurdles you master along the way instead of just waiting for the big ones that never seem to be enough. You'll know that you're awesome just for making the effort and understand that mistakes are par for the course. You'll adjust your relationship with your weight to a place where you accept yourself as whole and as worthy. You'll incorporate all of these practices and more, and coexist peacefully, joyfully, and consistently with food.

I wrote this book for you, my dear reader. It's my way of paying forward everything I've learned. Whatever dysfunctional relationship you have with food, it has most likely held you back from loving your true self. You will learn how to use your authentic voice, show it who's boss, and in doing so, flourish in countless areas. You can live a life where you will be liberated from constantly researching diets and obsessing about the numbers on a scale. You were meant to surpass this and come out victorious on the other side. Food does not need to have a hold over you indefinitely.

The courage that it took to write this book came from hope. Helping you through the messages on the following pages is a million times more important to me than protecting the vulnerability I feel revealing this part of me I've kept secret for so long. I wanted to open my heart to others who are going through the same things I endured, and offer assistance with the consequent realizations about a lifetime of my struggles with food. My healing and growth have helped me release my old story for a new, improved one. And that's what I wish for you.

Throughout this book, I share my journey of how I came to that place of being comfortable with food and with myself after more than forty years of trials and tribulations. I want to be completely transparent and make it abundantly clear that it's not as if I've "beat" binge eating and now it's gone from my life forever. Every day, I make conscious choices that bring me closer to living my best life. My story shows how the lessons I learned to make those choices appeared in my life one by one, slowly over time. First, I will take you through my journey of systematic awareness, desensitization to the stimuli of food, and the removal of the detrimental actions that no longer serve me. I will then guide you through how I painstakingly applied and incorporated one new, small principle until it became an organic part of my daily repertoire. Finally, I gained an intuitive awareness that I successfully incorporated into strategies and coping mechanisms. Are you ready to grab hold of them? You may have doubt or reservations, but the benefits will outweigh the risks.

We are going to break the bingeing cycle once and for all by discovering the true depths of your soul, and how you can step into your seismic power and take back your control. It's about believing you deserve more out of life, choosing to be positive, and applying the wisdom you gain to reach your goals. You will see evidence of the universal truth that we were put on this earth for a purpose so that we can achieve the highest level of spirituality possible. And most importantly, you will spend your life knowing your worth because you are a child of G-d, the heir of a King. Imagine that.

Now is the time to reach deep into your soul and commence yet another journey. I know you have the strength within you to change. So, buckle up and let's go. I thank you for the gift of allowing me to share my story with you.

CHAPTER 1

What Is a Binge?

I have heard every avoidance tactic known to man for taking control over what we put in our mouths. I'll control my eating:

"When things calm down."

"When I am less overwhelmed."

"When I can wrap my head around it."

"Maybe after the holidays."

"In the summer, which is better than now."

"When I am less exhausted."

"When my kids get settled."

"When I get more organized."

"But I just love food. Especially cookies."

"But I need to get motivated first."

The unfortunate truth is that there will never be a convenient time to change your relationship with food, and there is no better time than right now. Making the decision to put your foot down once and for all with erratic food habits and change your life for the better will never be convenient. If managing food consumption was easy and we had all the time in the world, everyone would look like an Instagram fitness model. But life will always be in session and is never a straight journey. There will always be obstacles, losses, hardships, disappointments, and difficulties. You feel overwhelmed, depressed, have fears of not being enough, and struggle to manage through illness or injury. You're tired, overworked, underpaid, unmotivated, euphoric, lacking emotion, or just plain ambivalent. The time will seemingly never be *now*.

And although you may truly believe that life's overwhelming circumstances give you a pass, here's the real deal: *none* of these reasons give you permission to shove an entire chocolate cake into your face. Or stop going to the gym, or overworking your business, or any counterintuitive action that takes you far away from positive participation toward your life's goals. Of course there will be times when you need to sit out a day, or go easy on yourself and take a walk instead of your usual intense weight-lifting workout. But "self-care" doesn't mean giving up on your health because life gets too overwhelming. You are worth more than just giving up. Dust yourself off and try again.

I am here to remind you of your greatness. Your birthright is not to be a slave to food. This is your formal invitation to lean in and become the person you were meant to be. The cake—or whatever you use to soothe yourself—is not your friend. It will only make matters worse because your clothes won't fit and you will look at yourself in the mirror and wonder what on G-d's green earth causes you to keep overeating. Why do you keep coming back to the comfort that ironically causes you the most discomfort? Because you do not yet believe you are worth it. I wasn't clear I was worth it. I am clear now, but it took me over forty years to get to that place.

I have named my food issue *binge and sprint*. While no two people's binges are exactly alike, bingeing universally is an exercise in futility that you use to make yourself feel better that just ends up making you feel worse. So you overeat again to make yourself feel better, and round and round you go without fruition. You think you're using it to center yourself, but it only serves to throw you completely off-kilter. Every time. Without exception.

Dr. Sacker defines *binge eating* as a type of eating disorder where you eat a large amount of food in a short amount of time without feeling hungry. You can experience a lack of control of what or how much you are eating. The emotional state includes shame, guilt, embarrassment, and the desire to hide by eating in secrecy. Negative body image and self-hatred can further enhance emotional stress, depression, and anxiety.

You may read my forthcoming description of a binge and say, "That's it? This girl's got nothing on me." Or maybe you'll think, "Woah. I'm not nearly as bad as she is, and I feel so much better about myself after reading that!" But I promise you will find enough similarities in the thoughts and actions behind my eating habits to at least glean a few golden nuggets that will help you on your continued journey to freedom.

If there was a hidden camera in my kitchen, here's what it would show:

I hurry into the kitchen immediately after experiencing some sort of discomfort. Maybe I was just given a large task to do. Perhaps a phone call made me feel upset. I'm alone, clearly on some sort of mission, and my expression reads determined, perturbed, and glazed over all at once. It's written all over my face that I have a million things going on in my mind, and I feel completely unsettled because something or everything has been uncomfortable. I open the cabinets and fridge in quick succession, removing the oddest of combinations of the highest caloric foods I can find. My movements are quick and frantic. I clearly have no idea where to start to fill the void and stuff the undesired feeling. I can't calm down, and then the business of eating starts. I stand at the counter, of course. Bowls of cereal with milk and drizzled honey and handfuls of chocolate chips thrown in. My kids' snacks for school dipped in almond butter. Anything resembling cake. And then salty. Cheese of all kinds. Margarine on stale crackers. Expired cream cheese on frozen waffles. My brain is completely removed from my body as if something has taken over my actions and I'm working on instinct or being programmed by some alien planet.

When I do a binge, here are the types of thoughts that run through my head: *Help me! What can I put in my body that will calm me down? No, wait, I'm bigger than this. This won't help me. I can stop right now. I can't stop. I'll just have this little bit. This will make me feel better. I'll start again tomorrow.*

I really do try to stop, but the pull to food is just so powerful and I'm no match for its strength. Sometimes, I'm completely on autopilot and can think of nothing but what food is in the next cabinet. Anything to stuff that overwhelming feeling. It's messy, and my stomach hurts, and it's a massive waste of time, which is ironic because I'm often stressed about not having enough time. I'm clearly trying to pull myself together and falling apart in the process.

Eventually, I begin to slow down, but it's not because I'm finally satiated. The truth is that I can only fit so much in my body at one time. I see evidence of the binge in empty wrappers and crumbs, but nine times out of ten I couldn't tell you what I ate. Then the mind unclenches and the binge fog lifts. I am bloated and stuffed and think, *Okay, I'm relaxed now. My mind isn't racing like it was, and I can look at things objectively and calmly and decide what to do next.* Meaning I'm exhausted from the binge and lost in a gluten fog. Sometimes that means I've truly calmed my brain down sufficiently to think a bit more clearly, but it's usually rare that I have clarity. Whatever the outcome, it only temporarily reduces the enormity of what I'm facing until the next overwhelming thought takes over and I use food to quiet my mind and body from racing. It's not like I'm solving any problems. I am just numbing myself.

I've binged over issues both big and small since I was eight years old. The issue that catapults the binge may change, but the coping mechanism remains the same. I can't think what to do next, so I automatically turn to food to pull myself together by stuffing the feeling. And I never know how long it will last. Sometimes I'm back in the kitchen after five minutes. Sometimes after a week or even a year. Bouts of manic eating have lasted different amounts of time at different points in my life. I've had binges that lasted for an hour, for a week, for months, or even years. It depends on what I was going through and how much I needed to depend on food to get me through different challenges in my life. When times were particularly difficult, I overate several times a week over a period of a year, or even several years. Sometimes, just here and there would be enough. You can completely tell how I'm doing in my life by my dress size. No need to ask, "Hey, how are you?" You can just look at me and either say, "So glad you're doing fabulously," or "How can I help?"

After a particularly long bout of reaching for food in an unhealthy way, there are complicating factors. For one, I'm in a constant sugar coma, which diminishes my ability to think clearly and make good decisions for myself. My determination to succeed subsides, and now I'm an underachiever. In addition, I've gained so much weight that I don't even look like myself, which makes me feel awful. And I binge again.

I decided to ask some close friends who experienced similar struggles what most commonly initiated a binge session. Most people I posed this question to said, "When I'm stressed." I don't know about you, but I'm stressed a lot in my life. I mean, I'm not stressed out all day, but I'm usually stressed at some point every day. I asked them for clarification.

"What kind of stress? Good stress, bad stress, happy stress, family stress, work stress, getting-the-kids-on-the-bus stress, not-knowing-what-shoes-to wear-with-your-skinny-jeans stress . . ." The overwhelming answer? "I don't know. Just . . . stress." If you are at this point in your awareness around food, I feel your pain. I've been there for about forty years. You are not alone.

But after years of not knowing, with some guidance I've been able to slow down the process in my mind and become super aware of my feelings before, during, and after a binge. I've learned that I don't have to be happy or sad or bored or euphoric to use food in an unhealthy way. Those general mood categories don't really have anything to do with a binge for me. The stress I experience as a result of expectations is what causes me to binge most. When others expect something of me, when I expect something of myself, or when someone doesn't expect anything at all, but I think they do. The thought of it scares me. It started as a kid when I learned to use food as a catalyst to get me through emotional confusion with my family and friends. Like I did, you will need to look at your early years to discover what originally conditioned you to use food in an unhealthy way.

I also used food as the fuel to change direction instead of simply saying a prayer before I dive into a new challenge, conversation, or even a simple task. I had my spirituality at my fingertips my whole life, but instead I chose to engage in endless eating tirades to soothe me as I worked through tasks I didn't want to be doing at the time. I used food to "calm down" versus prayer (which has no calories, by the way). I used food to fill a void so I could approach a situation with strength when, in fact, G-d was all around me. I used food to focus so I could successfully think what to do next when all I was doing was creating more turmoil.

Then there is the most nonsensical reason why I binged: to signify the end of a previous binge. I used food to steady myself so I could move on. The food grounded me, almost like a place marker in time. For example, I may justify a binge in this way: "I'm feeling this feeling, or bingeing on this food, or doing this activity now, so this muffin will mark the fact that I'm now transitioning to another feeling or activity, and I can now move on from where I don't want to be to where I do want to be."

Does all or any of my "binge logic" sound familiar to you? Take a moment to identify all the areas you use food to fill a gap, soothe an emotion, or ease a transition. If you can't think of one immediately, start noticing when you do it. Maybe you're working at your computer when a new task comes on the horizon. Perhaps this task gives you some unease or has unknowns attached to it. Suddenly, baking cookies or eating the last ice cream bar sounds like a very good idea. A soothing idea to help you ponder as you get over the hump. Using cake as fortitude. Let me tell you, the pondering you are doing is actually laced with anxiety because that is what is ultimately driving you to food.

Overeating also made me feel constructive. It made me feel good because I was *busy doing* something instead of just letting a negative feeling eat at me (pun intended). A task that I could complete. And once I'm done, I'm satiated on many different levels. After that particular feeding frenzy moment is over, I'm temporarily numbed enough to the discomfort that launched the overeating in the first place, and then I can move on to whatever comes next for me in my day. It was my strength even though it was destroying my life the entire time. It was my drug, a true addiction.

Food was the comfort I employed to ease my discomfort. The food refueled me as it delivered me into a different, more relaxed state away from the chaos and frenzy I couldn't escape on my own. Just a little push to get me through the day. All I had to do was stick the proverbial needle into my vein and allow the food to take its course, and I'd be back to achieving and feeling fine in a jiffy. I used food to handle innocuous and arduous situations.

Eventually, I successfully trained myself to cope with life without abusing food. Yes, there have been setbacks, but I now have an arsenal of strategies born out of many years of experiences and lessons learned. I call on them to get myself back on track to my now consistently healthy lifestyle. I will show you how you can do the same.

There are other categories of overeating as well, and we all do them.

- Mindlessly "picking" at the picnic or party.
- Starving and grabbing the first thing you see.
- Craving a particular food in a moment of weakness.
- Sitting in a CVS parking lot stuffing your face with Reese's Peanut Butter Cups.
- Fatigue eating as a stimulant to stay awake.
- Bored eating.
- Sad eating.
- Nervous eating.
- Procrastination eating.
- When you're out with friends.

The list is endless.

The Dark Voice

Think about the language we use when it comes to food.

"I was bad on my diet today."

"I was so good at the breakfast meeting this morning."

This type of self-talk—how we think about our food decisions, and how we reinforce it by using this disturbing dialect with our friends—reduces us back to our childhood. We say things like this to justify our decisions to ourselves. When we were small, we were incapable of making responsible decisions for ourselves and needed constant supervision. We took the word of higher authorities in our lives as scripture, no matter how wrong it was. We willingly gave over our power. For me, this created in my mind something I will be referring to in this book as my Dark Voice.

The Dark Voice lives in all of our heads. Its sole objective is to whisper in your ears that you're not worthy of the life you dream of. It grips and paralyzes your very being in its lying snare. You may not even realize it's there, but it's the one thing that stands between you and your dreams. It may seem like the only way to silence the Dark Voice is to binge. If you can slow down the negative messages in your head, I bet you have a Dark Voice too. The good news is that I'm going to help you see how that Dark Voice works. You will learn how to disarm it and free yourself from its tyranny.

I am a Modern Orthodox Jew. The way I define an Orthodox Jew is a Jewish person who lives their life practicing traditions and customs as defined by the Old Testament, such as keeping the Sabbath, Festivals, and the laws of eating Kosher food, among other things. I do talk about my experiences with binge eating within the context of the Jewish religion, and having faith in G-d at different points in this book. Please feel free to substitute "G-d" for "Higher Power," "Source Energy," "the Universe," "Jesus," "Allah," or whatever speaks to you. Regardless of what religion you identify with or don't identify with, the same thing that's happening around my table is happening around yours. My aunt Esther who prepares the brisket for Passover seder is the same as your aunt Mary who brings the ham to Christmas dinner, or your uncle Ed who insists on manning the barbecue on July 4.

But whatever sect of Judaism you may or may not be familiar with, the Jewish people love to eat for every occasion, and food is everywhere. Death, life, celebration, holidays, Sabbath on Friday night and Saturday. This can be a gift and a curse for me with food, yet it's still not an excuse to overeat because in my religion G-d loves me and wants me to love myself. Ironically, my religion, the most omnipresent spiritual thing in my life, seems to be working against me in the food arena.

Around every corner, religion throws different celebrations in your path that push you off your healthy eating game. Most Jewish holidays have the exact same theme. "They tried to kill us. We won. Let's eat." But you don't have to be an Orthodox Jew to understand what I'm saying. While I celebrate Sabbath *every* Friday night and Saturday—where the amount of food served rivals Christmas dinner—maybe you have huge Sunday dinners every week that derail you. We all have weddings, christenings, bar mitzvahs, engagement parties, vacations, business trips, happy hour, office parties, birthday parties, book club, a night out with the girls, and bake sales, not to mention the plethora of random events that pop up on any given Wednesday. Take all of that, plug it into the Holiday Calendar of Events that you celebrate, and you have a continual feast-a-thon your body is endlessly battling.

For me, there never appeared to be a good time to start a healthy eating regime because I was stuck in a year-round onslaught of food between the Jewish and American holidays. Then there is Eid, Kwanza, the Chinese New Year, Rosh Hashanah, Shavuot, Thanksgiving, and New Year's Eve thrown into the mix with Purim (which is particularly food crazy) and Passover (food insanity). I encounter massive meals and decadent snacks on what seems like 320 days out of the 365 days in a year. It seems like everything is working against me to keep my body fit and healthy to align with my soul. I turn to my religion to elevate me both physically and spiritually, but I concurrently get slammed with all this food. An ironic double-edged sword.

Take Purim, for example. There is no way for me to adequately describe the overwhelming amount of food that crosses your threshold during this holiday. You need to see it with your own eyes to believe it. One of the customs on this holiday is to deliver packages of food to your neighbor. And, of course, we wouldn't want to insult anyone by leaving them off the list! Add the fact that each of your kids is doing the same exact thing, and before you know it, an average family of five has prepared about sixty perfectly prepared packages of decadence to deliver. Do you know what the result of sixty packages going out is? You guessed it! Sixty packages of decadence *coming in*! They sit in temptation on your dining room table for you to open and sample throughout the day at your leisure. Or you start chowing down on them on the road if you're the one doing the deliveries as your kids eagerly hop in and out of the minivan to the next home. They arrive back at the car giddy, their eyes glazed over with sugar, tearing open the most recent bag they've procured. But wait, there's more! There is also a custom to have a feast toward the day's end. Yup, you read that right. I get together with my cousins for a potluck with extra desserts in addition to the packages of food exchanged between all of our households. On this holiday, there are no holds barred. For the most part, we don't even pretend to watch what we're eating.

Yet despite the odds stacked against me, I no longer use my religion as an excuse. I have committed to being around food in my religion and not falling flat on my face in cake. I have relaxed with food. I have leaned into my soul and found my self-worth. I'll never be perfect, but I do take 100 percent responsibility for what I put into my mouth. I no longer blame it on circumstance. I wish I could tell you this mature accordance with my rules of food happened overnight, but it took decades. Yet, here is the good news: because I suffered for so long, I can help you build a space of love for yourself so you can stop bingeing sooner.

I am not going to give you meal plans and exercises to do with resistance bands while you wait for carpool. I am going to give you the strategies and the mindset of believing you are worth the exercise and watching what goes into your mouth. This will get you to a mental place where your focus is not on the anxiety of who you are, but on the beauty and power of the intelligent, amazing, accomplished, fabulous *you*. Look, I'm all for having a plan that incorporates a way of eating that works for you. It provides structure, and I love structure because it gives me parameters to work within, and it makes me feel safe. There are so many fabulous, healthy ways to eat like vegan, Mediterranean, alkaline, raw, vegetarian, pescatarian, swearing off cake (I've actually met people who have declared swearing off cake. Forever. Personally, I don't get that one. I mean, how do you swear off cake? It's cake. Aren't you going to want cake at some point?) low fat, low protein, low carb, high carb . . . the list goes on forever. You can follow any of these to success, and that's great! Find the one that works best for your body and go for it. But if you're like me and you've tried everything out there and "nothing works for you," I promise it's not the method of eating you're following (or trying to follow, or not following at all). The methods work just fine. It's the Dark Voice in your head.

The Dark Voice will get you every time. As you read this book, the Dark Voice will creep up because it is sneaky and wants you to forget it exists. No meal plan or workout marathon will ever stabilize you in a place of soulful peace until you slay that dirt-sucking piece of garbage Dark Voice dead in its tracks. That's why so many of us use a food plan to lose a ton of weight only to gain it all back. The Dark Voice is still alive and well.

If you want to beat gaining and losing the same weight again and again permanently, the only way to succeed is to do all the mental heavy lifting. You have to unpack the past, the trauma, and the cues of why you're so stressed out about who you are in the first place. To allow your mind to have precedence over your body. It will help you cut through all the mental confusion of finding a way of eating that is perfect for you in a clear headspace where you understand your worth and your right to a healthy body. Once you really go through the process of getting your head clear, you will begin to build a life that naturally sustains healthy eating habits. You may even feel that food restrictions and specific food plans are no longer required. You'll be able to eat without the constant noise in your head: *Wait, did I measure that? Is it on my plan? Should I eat the bread? I said I was going to save my calories for dessert. But it's just this once. Ugh, I can't believe I did that.* There will still be some of it. I joined Weight Watchers about forty years ago with my mom, and I still mentally check off my boxes in each food category as I go about my day so I can be mindful of what and how much I'm eating. It's a great lifelong skill, and I'm grateful for it as it's helped keep me in check.

You can create a world where food isn't relied upon for anything other than nourishing your body and soul for your ultimate good. But you need to start right now because the longer you steep yourself into the bottomless pit of relying on food to soothe you, the further down you slide in every area of your life, and the harder it is to see yourself for who you really are: a child of G-d, the heir of a King. You will see that when you focus on improving the physical "you" for the soul that lies within, the result is a renewed sense of faith, and a deeper belief in both yourself and the higher power that holds you. The road ahead to your best self will be paved in the highest highs and the lowest lows, but in my experience the authentic, glorious you will be waiting at the end of it, making the journey all the worthwhile.

CHAPTER 2

Binge and Sprint

Now that we have addressed the binge, and I have blown the cover of the Dark Voice in your head that is always out to get you, let me introduce another concept: the *binge and sprint* method. Understanding the binge and sprint method is important to being successful on your journey of coming to terms with your body and your own personal overeating patterns.

First, you *binge*, or otherwise use food in an unhealthy way to give you the fortitude you need to get out there and accomplish whatever it is that you have your heart set on doing. From the simplest tasks to the impossible.

Next, you take the strength you got from bingeing and you *sprint*. The sprint is getting the tasks done at all costs with sheer brute force, an iron will, an unstoppable strength. You throw introspection out the window, practice zero self-care, fun not included, no joy required.

Now, don't get me wrong, I owe a lot to binge and sprint. Binge and sprint helped me lose weight many, many, many times (clearly, the bingeing was at a reduced level when losing weight, but it was still there). It got me A's in school. It got me a scholarship for a master's degree at an Ivy League university, and an acceptance for a full ride PhD to that same institution. It allowed me to build a very successful business while bringing up a young and busy family, while working a full-time job, among accomplishing countless other major milestones. But it also never really allowed me to go as far as I could in life, or enjoy my accomplishments that I worked so hard for, and it physically left me a complete mess. It was so often fueled by the need to squash that uncomfortable feeling over and over again versus asking myself why the feeling kept coming up in the first place. But telling you my story doesn't make the truth, or facts, or abuse of food go away.

We all need to start at the beginning. This is your cue to reflect upon your own generational patterns. Keep them in mind as you read about my family history, because one must look at their own past to rebuild in the present.

I developed the binge-and-sprint method slowly over my entire life and applied it to everything I did because, as we all well know, how you do anything is how you do everything. My dad modeled binge and sprint for me growing up. One hand encircled and protected the food on his plate and the other brought the food to his mouth as quickly as possible. He was a fast eater. Hands down, an all-time Olympic gold medalist of fast eating. You would think there were a herd of antelopes right behind his chair, and their fate depended on whether or not he finished his meal before a pack of lions pounced on them. And if he didn't finish his meal before the lions caught up to the antelopes, *bam!* He would share their fate. It was truly an amazing sight. If asked why he didn't slow down and enjoy his food, he would reply, "I grew up on Pitt Street. If you didn't eat fast, there would be nothing left." A typical response for a binge and sprinter. No time for enjoying and connecting with your body and the eating experience. Just get it done and move on to the next task with abandon.

My dad had a history of sprinting. Born in 1933 on New York City's Lower East Side during Prohibition, the Great Depression, and the beginnings of World War II, food was scarce and sacred for his generation, and it was a selfish, insulting sin and globally insensitive to leave anything unfinished on your plate. Children of his generation were constantly scolded that "Children are starving in Europe!" My dad had his first job at five years of age (he was a singer, among other things, but more about that later). In his adult life, he would wake every day at 5:00 a.m. and leave our house on Staten Island a half an hour later. He took a bus, a ferry, and several subways to work as a social worker at a nursing home in the Bronx, and returned at 7:20 p.m. He ate dinner in record time (no surprise there), and then at 7:45 the doorbell would ring and the litany of bar mitzvah boys (he was also a rabbi) would be ushered in and out for their lessons over the next few hours. On Sundays, he would leave the house early to teach religion at Hebrew School and perform graveside funeral ceremonies, which he would also squeeze into his lunch hour during the week. He completed a master's degree while working full time, and he hustled a million other ways to make a dollar for his family. Those dollars added up, and while my family was frugal, I never had to worry about taking care of my parents financially in their golden years.

How my dad managed binge and sprint was screaming. Lots of screaming. Fears of lack frustrated him, and because he was never shown how to deal with feelings, he yelled. The yelling in my home was frightening, and it debilitated me. But for my dad it was just, well . . . a mode of communication. He saw it as an effective way to express urgency. To him, his screaming meant nothing other than blowing off a little steam and relating to others what he needed, and that he needed it *now*. His yelling made it seem as though he needed to get his needs met in that very instant or the world may, in fact, blow up.

So, stuffing my feelings through binge and sprint was passed down to me through my DNA. If my dad could have slowed down and busied himself with some introspection, life might have been much more enjoyable, effective, and even more successful for him. I can only imagine how far he could have gone. Just the thought of what his Dark Voice must have said to him makes me want to cry.

The screaming and yelling in my home during my childhood never failed to terrify me. Yet it was in the midst of one of these screaming marathons, of all places, that I saw a glimmer of what my worth could be. I was almost eight years old, and on that particular night the yelling was nonstop. I dragged all of the stuffed animals off my bed and piled them on top of me on the bottom of my sister Sarah's closet to drown out the screaming. I lay there for what seemed like forever until I heard the bedroom door open. *Oh no! Who was it? Was the yelling going to start in this room? Was I going to have to find another hiding spot?* The closet door opened, and before I knew what was happening, the stuffed animals were pulled off me with lightning speed. My sister Mimi, who had just turned thirteen, came to find me to make sure I was okay. My hero. She helped me to my feet and led me into the bathroom, the only room in the house with a lock on it that could offer us the assured privacy we sought. I started to cry.

The bathroom was small and narrow and yellow. It was dimly lit as only the nightlight was on. We both stood and faced the mirror over the vanity. Mimi stood behind me and gently ran a brush though my hair as we listened to what we should definitely not have been hearing.

"What's happening now—this screaming—this is not your

life," Mimi said. "You are only here because you're a kid, and you don't have a choice. But one day when you grow taller and stretch out, you'll lose some weight, you'll outgrow your pimples, and you will be able to choose whoever you want to marry. You will be so beautiful, and you will have your pick of anyone. Then you will have choices, and you can make your life any way you want it to be. So don't be sad because this is only temporary. It's not *your* life."

My sister was thirteen and knew what was up. Not exactly politically correct, but hey, it was the seventies, and pretty practical and accurate advice for that time. I left that bathroom with two invaluable gems: a seed of hope for a bright future had been planted, and knowing that my sister was an angel watching over me.

I was the little girl Mimi was referencing in the mirror. I was an unpopular, overweight, pimple-faced, oily-haired girl who had the misfortune of developing earlier than anyone else. Even at an early age, I was so busy moving, and never resting it was as if my body said, "Come on! Hurry up and grow already! Don't just sit around doing nothing! Let's get the show on the road! Move!"

For the entire week prior to my eighth birthday, my parents told me they had a special surprise for me. Every chance they got, there were winks and elbow nudges and secret smiles. I was literally jumping out of my skin with excitement. *Something special just for me! Was it a Barbie house? A new jump rope? Piano lessons? Maybe it was the same bicycle bell my neighbor Lorraine had.* I could put it on the yellow bike with the banana seat that I inherited from my sister.

Finally, the day came. My sisters, Sarah and Mimi, made me a corsage with eight sugar cubes dangling from pipe cleaners that were attached to a white bow. I wore it proudly in school all day. I felt so special. I ran home from the bus and couldn't wait for dinner to be over so I could open my present. I jumped out of my seat when my mother brought it into the kitchen. It was a small box. Well, good things come in little packages, right? I carefully took off the wrapping paper. With a huge smile that clearly conveyed all of the birthday magic I had in my eight-year-old heart, I carefully pulled the blue ball of fluff out of the box. And there it was. Something was hanging from it. It was gold. Was it a necklace? No . . . The blue fluffy ball was actually a keychain. With a key.

Huh.

Was it a skate key? Was I getting new roller skates? No, this one had teeth.

It was too big to be a key for a special private diary, or one of those jewelry boxes where you opened it and a perfect, delicate ballerina would spin to a beautiful melody.

My confused look gave way to my parents' outpouring of excited explanation.

"It's your very own key to the house, big girl! Happy birthday!"

I was baffled. *Why would I need a key to the house,* I remember thinking. My mother was home when I got off the bus, but if she was at work, I went to the Gordons' down the block. They always had Girl Scout Tagalong cookies, the peanut butter ones covered in chocolate. Oh man, I can still taste them. No wonder I liked going there. Come to think of it, I definitely ate way too many cookies there. At the time, I wondered if that was the reason why my parents gave me a house key. Maybe the Gordons thought I ate too many of their cookies and they didn't want me around anymore.

"Mommy is now going to be coming home from work a bit later each and every Wednesday," my mother said. "I'm going to come home just a half hour after you do, and now that you're eight and such a big girl, you're big enough to come home by yourself!"

No, I'm not. I was only seven yesterday, I thought.

"Starting when?" I asked.

"Tomorrow! Isn't that great?"

No.

"Why can't I just go down the block to the Gordons' to play with Celia on Wednesdays like I always do?"

"Because you're big now! We told all of the neighbors, and they are all going to watch you go from the bus to the house and make sure you get in safely."

Oh no. My stomach didn't feel right. Everyone was smiling, but I didn't like what was happening. Coming home alone in the dark sounded really scary. I didn't want to be alone. *What if I promised Mrs. Gordon I wouldn't eat so many cookies,* I remembered thinking.

"Come! Let's go downstairs and practice opening the door with your shiny new key!"

It was then that I realized that no matter what I said, nothing would change. My stomach sank. It had already been decided. At the time, I truly believed the Gordons didn't want me anymore because I ate too much, and that it was all my fault. I vowed to never eat cookies again (which clearly did not last too long). I associated being separated from others as a result of my eating too much, which started a cycle of self-imposed bouts of isolation during and after abusing food. It started a pattern of shamefully overeating in secret, followed by putting *myself* into solitary confinement, just like this experience taught me to do. Unfortunately, like most children, I was a really great observer, but due to my young development, I was limited in interpreting the real meaning behind the message.

The next day was my voyage into independence. I got off the bus, feeling excited and nervous. I turned the key like my mom had shown me the night before, scooted into the house as quickly as I could, whipped around, slammed the door shut, and locked it behind me.

It was so quiet.

"Hello?"

There was no answer. I instantly felt the heaving in my chest and the hot feeling in my face as tears welled up in my eyes.

No! I thought. *I'm big now. I'm responsible, and I'm allowed to stay in the house by myself.*

Determined not to let my parents down and to prove to them that they could depend on me, I turned on the lights, hung up my coat, and climbed the stairs with my knapsack to the kitchen. I felt panicked. I searched my brain for something that would calm me down. "Keep moving, do something constructive," was the answer I received.

I see now I had the Dark Voice when I was eight years old, and my go-to for my low self-worth and self-sabotage has been food. But at the time I thought moving and doing was the best idea because I was always taught that if I kept moving and doing, it would keep me out of trouble at home. I even received praise for it. That was what I always saw my father do—come home, eat dinner quickly, and sprint to do all things constructive. No time for relaxing! Fill your down time! It was the perfect setup, passed down to me in my very nervous system. That very moment marked the start of a lifetime of equating relaxation and stillness as slothful and ungainly. I used constant movement, work, and gorging myself with food to stifle anxiety, emotions of all kinds, expectations, and most everything in my life. Don't feel, just stuff it and move. Binge and sprint. If my father did it, it must be right!

What about you? Take a moment to identify when you use food for anything other than nourishment for your highest good. Where did you learn to do that, and how did it start? Make this connection now and take it with you as you travel with me on this journey. Allow the synapses to open your eyes to your own destructive food patterns and their source as we travel through the next forty years of my battle with bingeing. Together, through the trials and tribulations, we will learn what it takes to break that connection so you, too, can be free.

Back in the kitchen, alone at eight years old, armed with my new "sprint" outlook on life, I thought, *All right, I'm on the right track*. I instantly felt safer. My parents always told me I was a good girl when I was "doing." But I wondered what should I be doing. My thoughts led me to what I did when I went to the Gordons' house after school. I ate cookies.

I opened the cabinet, but there were no cookies. I opened the freezer where my mom usually kept some brownies she would bake in advance in case we had unexpected company. Nothing. I went back to the cabinet. There was an unopened box of Cap'n Crunch cereal.

"Well, I guess this will have to do," I said.

I took out a bowl and my special "breakfast" spoon. It was a yellow plastic spoon that said "Have a good breakfast" on the handle that I got as a prize in a box of Trix cereal. I poured the cereal and the milk into the bowl, then sat down on the white wrought-iron kitchen chair with the aqua plastic cushions. I put that first delicious spoonful in my mouth and instantly relaxed. It felt so right. It filled all my criteria of what I should be doing as a big, responsible girl all alone in the house. I was sticking to a routine, doing something constructive and not just sitting there—I mean, you have to eat, right? I felt very adult-like eating a meal by myself. When I finished, I looked down into the empty bowl; there was so much milk left over. I couldn't put it back in the fridge for later or it would taste yucky, and I couldn't waste it. I thought about adding more cereal so that I didn't waste the milk. I wasn't really hungry, but it gave me something constructive to do so I wouldn't just be sitting there, and I wouldn't have time to cry, which would disappoint my parents. I poured in the cereal, and once again, that first bite relaxed my body and made me feel so much better. I ate that cereal like someone was chasing me.

I learned that food would keep me safe, preoccupied, and away from fear. If I was ever afraid of something, I could just eat and it would make me feel better. I didn't fully understand the mindset, the Dark Voice in my head, that was being formed at eight years old, or that my abuse with food originated from both my father's example of stuffing then sprinting, as well as the fact that doing all things constructive would abate his yelling, which terrified me, but that's the moment the seed was planted. When I was eating, it literally filled me. It made me "more." It made me "enough." And that knowledge calmed me and made me feel like I was good, or more accurately, "good enough" so that the yelling would stop. In my eight-year-old understanding, I believed that my father yelled because I was not "doing," and therefore not "being good enough." But because he didn't yell when I was busy "doing," then I would just follow his model and binge and sprint forever to keep myself safe. What I didn't know at the time was that the sprint would be a forty-year marathon.

I don't remember how many bowls of cereal I ate. But I do remember wanting another bowl. As I reached for more cereal, I realized the box of Cap'n Crunch that I'd just opened was now empty. *Empty? Oh no, Mommy will be so angry. She just bought this box.* All of a sudden, I didn't feel responsible anymore. I felt irresponsible, bad, and ashamed, completing the perfect circle of what I have come to learn that so many of us do. It was the downswing of the binge-and-sprint cycle. It was the immediate disproval of the "good enough" feeling I hoped would calm me and keep me safe. The binge cycle cruelly crushed the self-worth I sought to uplift, the very opposite of what I hoped it would do.

In a panic that I would be found out, I dug out half the garbage, placed the empty box in the middle, and put the rest of the garbage on top of it, burying the evidence. I quickly put the milk back in the fridge, washed and dried my bowl and special yellow plastic breakfast spoon, and put them away. No sooner had I closed the cutlery drawer did I hear the front door open.

"I'm home!"

Mommy! Oh happy day! Mommy is home!

"I'm upstairs," I said in a calm, grown-up voice.

"Oh, my big girl!" She hugged me with all her might.

"I let myself in the house. I was so big and so responsible!"

"Yes, you were! I'm so proud of you!"

She gave me a beaming smile. I could see the relief in her face that she would be able to count on me so that she could bring in more money that she needed to support us. She was such a good mother, doing her best for us.

"Well, my big girl," she continued. "You must be starving. Help me get dinner on the table and tell me about your day at school."

I kept smiling at her, but there was panic behind the facade. How on earth would I be able to eat dinner? I felt like I was going to throw up. But I couldn't tell her and let her down. I needed to play along.

I went to bed that night feeling like my stomach was going to rip right open, but I was also pleased that I could stay home alone and do what my family needed. I was proud of myself even though my coping mechanisms led me to believe that a healthy, beautiful body comes only second to the needs of others. My bingeing became something I could rely on to help me live up to expectations, even though it brought destruction and shame. Cereal and milk became my routine every Wednesday.

I quickly generalized my newly acquired coping mechanism of using food to deal with stress into every area of my life. I was hooked, but my new frame, teetering on the fence between chubby and overweight, presented some new problems and invited unwanted attention. I was referred to much of the time as "pleasantly plump" by other adults. My family gave me a new nickname in my house: "Fatty." Really. Fatty. Not that it was unwarranted. I remember the night that nickname was given. I cried myself to sleep, but after a time, the name no longer stung. It became fact and part of my identity. It was just who I was. A truth. It became me.

From that time on, I began to analyze the innerworkings of other families, searching for other people who had gone through what I went through. But as I searched over time, I realized I was more alone than I thought. I discovered that the families I was closest to did not behave like mine. There was no scary screaming at my best friend Melissa's house. Lois and Henry were like second parents to me. I was at their house all the time, and it always felt so safe. You could relax out in the open without consequence. There was always someone to greet Melissa and me when we got off the bus when I went there after school. Her dad was a high school history teacher and was always ready to lend a hand with homework. I thought it was bizarre. I had never seen anyone get such in-depth help with their homework before. Everyone in my house was busy moving and doing their own work. I was aghast. I was sure it was cheating and that I should *not* be doing that. And then after homework, he asked us what we wanted for dinner. There were actual choices about what we wanted to eat. Huh, imagine that—being still for long enough in your own body to reflect on what it was that you wanted to eat at that moment. I felt like an alien that suddenly landed on a strange planet observing their life forms. And everything was "nice" in that house, even the food.

Henry would ask, "How about a nice steak with a nice salad for dinner?"

Bizarre. But I liked it . . . a lot.

I was never a fabulous athlete to begin with, and if not for Melissa, who was by far the best athlete in the school and therefore captain of choosing teams for every sport, I would have spent my entire grade school career being chosen last at every recess. The extra weight I had packed on made my running and coordination even slower than usual, and Melissa started taking some pretty heavy slack from some of the better players for choosing me at all. Eventually, my newly learned pattern of separating myself from those I felt unworthy to be around kicked in. I left those games and found comfort in a club my friend Annie made called "X-Cookies," or what I now realize was "No-Cookies so we can lose weight." It was my very first "diet/exercise" club.

We would run circles around the schoolyard, stopping at the steps after each lap to catch our breath. I never had to feel the shame of not getting chosen again for the skinny-girl games, but running away is not the answer. Sprint is not the answer.

If my story of the little girl who was excluded from social activities due to weight resonates with you, I can tell you that you no longer need to be your past. You were created as you were to live the best life and have a blast doing it. Seriously. That's it. We were not put here to suffer, feel less than, or drag around a self that doesn't fit. And if you've ever felt like retreating into a big box of cookies in solitude, be kind to yourself, open your eyes, and know that this is just conditioning for exclusion.

When you are still identifying with your past image, you're out of alignment with who you really are and what you deserve. You begin to compare your journey to others, and in watching everyone else's successes, you lose sight of your own vision of your future and your own special brand of how to creatively get there. You fruitlessly try and copy what other people are doing, and in doing so, you get further from your goals and your vision, and therefore feel even more separate from the people you originally compared yourself to because you'll never be them. And the more you do it, the more you get out of alignment with your higher power and the person you were meant to be, and the lower your self-worth drops. Why does this identifying with your past image take such a strong hold of you? Because it's the culmination of years of conditioning that started way before you were even born. It's taking what you learned growing up from past generations and needlessly adopting it as your own identity. Just like I did with my dad.

As a parent myself, I know I'm going to give my kids baggage. I'm just praying it's not going to be a steamer-trunkful. I'm hoping to pass on something more along the lines of a light backpack, or perhaps a small evening clutch. While it may seem as though my parents had no time for problems or just didn't care, I assure you that neither of these conjectures are true. It's important to understand the circumstances surrounding your parents' childhoods because your binge-and-sprint conditioning is deeper and wider than just your mother and father. It goes back to the ancestors before them. Both of my parents grew up in New York City during World War II and were the children of European immigrants who had close relatives that were being slaughtered by the Nazis. Their lives were not ones of leisure where people spoke about their feelings. It was a life where you were busy with the act of survival, and if you had a roof over your head, food on the table, and clothes on your back, then there was nothing to complain about.

My mother's father died when she was ten, and her mother passed when she was twenty-one. My mother's bedroom was the living room couch, and her closet was a hook on the back of a door. She gave up college to work and help her mother with the expenses. But my mom never talked about how hard things were. She talked about meeting up with her friends, and how the entire neighborhood would pile into her aunt Hannah's apartment to watch *Howdy Doody* because she had the first television on the block.

My father never had a childhood. When he wasn't in school, he was helping his dad at the barbershop or working instead of playing stickball in the street, or what people of those times referred to as the "gutter," with the other kids. From age six to fourteen, he was a mezzo-soprano and in such high demand that my grandfather finally had to hire a manager for him who booked him clear through every weekend. While all the fame and high pay he received may sound glamorous, my father sacrificed the person he wanted to be and the things he wanted to do for the benefit of others. Turns out binge and sprint isn't just about food. My dad's binge and sprint applied to ditching enjoyment and relationships to work himself into the ground, using professional and personal pursuits as a springboard to prove his worth, among an endless myriad of ways that he denied himself the joys of life. I was just like my father in this regard. So even when it was safe to finally relax, we both found that early conditioning made this impossible. Only work was for us. Frivolous enjoyment went against our grain and was reserved for the deserving folk of this world—a category we both knew we did not belong to. And if we ever momentarily forgot our place, our Dark Voices would soon remind us.

People of my parents' generation were fighters. They were practical. They never procrastinated. They didn't complain. They did not look beyond themselves for help. They also didn't pause for self-introspection regarding unresolved issues from their childhoods. And they certainly did not talk about their feelings. Could I blame my parents for not finding a better way to care for me? Sure. Could I hold on to my childhood pain and keep running from it? Of course. But why? Forgiveness is a journey to help you grow into the person you were meant to be. It won't come easy. It didn't for me. My story takes me all the way into the pit of the past and back again.

Let this seed be planted here and now for *you*. You are not your circumstances. You are not defined by your past experiences, the house you grew up in, your economic status, your education level, your jeans size, or mistakes you've made along the way. We all start out in life as diamonds in the rough. We all have sad stories. We don't need to be dominated by our pasts driving our Dark Voice. You can say *no* to what the Dark Voice is telling you to do and believe.

I'm asking you to stand up and declare this with me: "I am thrilled that this is the story of my life because I know that I was sent the exact challenges that I needed to become the person I was meant to be. I know that I can't blame my parents, or my circumstances, or the box of donut holes, or my third-grade teacher forever!" This life is about pulling yourself up by your fabulous, blinged-out bootstraps and basking in the glory of taking complete and utter responsibility for every single thing that happens in your life. And when that happens, you regain your power and that power sets you free.

I, for one, am down on my knees, kissing the ground with gratitude for every seemingly awful, horrible experience I've ever had because it led me to you. Without my experiences, I would not have started my business, or finished graduate school, or married my husband, or had my three incredible children who have grown with talents and challenges of their own. I owe all the joy, success, and continued growth in my life to binge and sprint, the Dark Voice, forty years of subsequent insane eating patterns, and everything that came along with it. The reason I am thankful is because my lifelong journey of struggle has forced me to face my downfalls and weaknesses, and understand and analyze them. In doing so, I've been able to flip them on their heads and use them to my advantage and beat them at their own game. You can do the same. You don't have to be a prisoner to a warden who doesn't care about your welfare, or Krispy Kreme Donuts, or an unhealthy relationship with anything or anyone. I'm holding your hand. We are doing this together. You are incredible. You are deserving. You are worthy.

Think back to when you knew your worth, before you learned from others to hide your bold, fabulous self. To when you were little and you lived out loud, unabashed and free from the Dark Voice, from food having control over you, and all your self-worth was intact. What were you like?

I am reminded of this question every Friday when I make challah bread for Sabbath.

Prior to shaping the dough into braids, a small piece is taken and burned in the oven to symbolize the sacrifices given to the High Priests in the times of the Holy Temple. There is a beautiful verse in the prayer that accompanies this ritual:

> *Just as giving the challah to the High Priest in former times served to atone for sins, so may it atone for mine, and I will be like a young child born anew. May it enable me to observe the holy Sabbath with my husband (and our children) and to become imbued with its holiness.*

While I understand that the point of this passage is to compare us to a child without sin, I often wonder if the real intention of this prayer is something a bit different. Perhaps it is referring to a child whose soul is yet unfettered by circumstance that causes him to forget his perfection and restrict his limitlessness. Because only such a child can best connect to G-d and therefore most effectively deliver this offering. A child who is himself without burden or unnecessarily weighty responsibility or doubt, free to live in the beautiful, authentic brightness of the higher power within him. Perhaps becoming like that child once again is, in fact, what we are praying for.

CHAPTER 3

Staying Ahead of the Curve

I personally know many women who seem to have it all. The ideal relationship, perfect kids, a beautiful home, an exciting career. It seems they have everything, but under the surface, their aspirations to truly embody their ideal physical selves are consistently depleted. No matter how smart, successful, and accomplished they are in all other areas of their lives, the vision of their healthier, fitter selves eludes them every time. Food is that one thing they just can't beat. These winners are forever comparing themselves to their thinner peers, wondering why the secret skinny file never crosses their desks, and in the process they separate themselves further from their power and their ultimate goal of living their best lives.

On the flipside of that, I was once privy to a conversation between two very successful women who were conjecturing as to why a different group of women were at the top of their industries and slim. Their conclusion? Because those women are "committed," and if you're able to remain committed in one area of your life, then you're committed in all areas of your life. I tried not to laugh. My first thought was that the successful women who were having this conversation had been thin their whole lives and clearly had no idea what they were talking about, so G-d bless them and their bikini-perfect figures. In my experience, if commitment was the only thing you needed to become relaxed in your body and comfortable with your worth, then many of us would already be supermodels. Having commitment is one thing, but implementing it is another. If you are as frustrated as I was about why you aren't where you want to be with your health, take solace as we are about to uncover yet more key skills and ideas you can take with you on your quest toward your healthiest life.

My upbringing *was* all about getting things done, commitment, stamina, and an ironclad work ethic, and I rose to the occasion every time. But my weight was the one battle I couldn't win because deep down I believed I was in the category of "have nots" that didn't deserve it. My dad often spoke about how we were different from those wealthier, prominent, respected, more successful families in our neighborhood. "Yeah, *they* get the honor in synagogue, but *we* don't." Or, "Sure, *they* can go on vacation, but *we* can't." And I obediently and voluntarily adapted this viewpoint when it came to my dress size, albeit subconsciously. "Sure, *other women* deserve to be slim, but *I* don't." I believed that I would never be enough no matter how hard I worked, how much I accomplished, or how many accolades I collected. But what I didn't know then was that if you can commit to a job, a business, a relationship, or learning how to do a cartwheel at forty, then you can commit to building a life of being with food in a healthy way. The trick is to unearth those beliefs that were buried deep in your soul at a young age that made you think that you were anything less than a perfect, deserving child of G-d. Kick that nonsense to the curb right now. Doing so will help you make the massive commitment you'll need to turn your life around and to get to that place of really knowing who you are. As it turns out, those successful women were right in that I'd be flexing the commitment muscle big time on my quest toward a healthy life.

With my committed upbringing, I started working different jobs at a young age, getting in sprint position early to not have to face the weight. When we were kids, there was zero tolerance for loafing about. In my house, we were always busy *doing*. My first real job was working for my sister Mimi when I was about ten. She was fifteen and had a custom crocheting business. She taught me how to do the work and then gave me the easier jobs. She was the big teenager who was the front for the business, and I was the ugly troll they hid in the attic doing the work. How could she charge fifty dollars for a finished product in 1978 done by a ten-year-old? I would sit on the rust-colored shag carpeting in our den and crochet and watch shows like *The Little House on the Prairie*, *The Waltons*, *The Love Boat*, and *Fantasy Island*. If I took a break to watch the next scene, my mom would lovingly yell, "Work!" If my dad caught us taking a break, his catch phrase, "Do something constructive," would snap us back into activity. In those early years, I was involved in many jobs: youth group leader, babysitter, camp counselor, pool lifeguard, short order cook at the Student Union building between classes, retailer at The Limited in the Staten Island Mall, and a million other things. As an adult, I have never had less than two or three jobs at once. When I was in the first years of growing my network marketing business and creating that tsunami of momentum, people would say, "Oh, that Naomi Joseph, she's a machine! Naomi, you're a machine!" And they were right. That old stamina kicked in, put the pedal to the metal, and mercilessly ran me into the ground. Sure, it served me as it got me to where I wanted to go, but I crashed, burned, and was totaled for years.

By the time I started my sophomore year of college, everything I did and every choice I made came down to sprint because that kept the weight down. I tried anorexia and bulimia. Anorexia lasted until lunch. Bulimia . . . I hated throwing up. Binge eating was my coping mechanism, like it or not. My life revolved around my weight—how I could lose more of it, how I could get smaller, and how I could look skinnier. It was the motivation for how I spent my time, money, and energy. My obsession with my body and food affected all of my decisions: what friends I made, what clubs I joined, how I socialized, what books I read, and what occupied the square footage of my mind.

To clarify, my drive to be more—which is less in body weight—was not rooted in the self-aware, healthy acceptance sort of way that you read about in personal development books. Nope. This obsession was born from not understanding my worth. The Dark Voice inside my head led me to believe that I was chopped liver if I wasn't at my goal weight. At that point in my life, I was in a race of applying binge and sprint to get as skinny as humanly possible. This balancing act—which wasn't balanced at all—was controllable, or so I thought. The little girl with the cereal box grew into a woman who had a solid purpose for her over-the-top behaviors.

I chose exercise above going out with friends, parties, dates, and study groups. I was committed and could see nothing else. I was treating the process of getting thin like a full-time job. In college, while people were packing on the study weight, I spent hours at the gym, jogging every chance I could get, trying several different weight loss programs, and weighing and measuring every morsel of food that entered my mouth.

The upside to all of this was that the more exercise I did, the better I felt. And the better I felt, the less I wanted to eat. And the less I ate, the skinnier I got, which only served to entrench my thinking that being skinny was the ultimate path to be on. Girls my age were supposed to be finding a husband, so I had to get skinny.

There was peer pressure to look as good as the other girls, so I had to get skinny. Forget raising my inner self. I wasn't looking to find the reason behind the bingeing. Taking time for introspection was way too self-indulgent. I just needed to keep moving and get skinny.

The stamina from sprint landed me on the Brooklyn College swim team. Practices were held twice daily: mornings before dawn when I wasn't doing anything anyway (Who needs sleep? What a waste of time!), and right after my last class ended, so I still had time to get home to help my mother with dinner. Yes, I was still living at home at that time, as did most nice Jewish girls in the neighborhood who went to local college.

The problem was that I was still in the midst of all the arguing and conflict that caused me the anxiety to overeat in the first place. I had been the only child at home for a few years since both of my sisters moved out. I was living in the same environment under the same conditions with the same triggers that taught me binge and sprint in the first place: my screaming father, and the rule that you must always be busy doing something constructive. No matter how hard I worked to get where I wanted, I had the underlying belief that I would never be good enough, and I would never be slim enough. I would need to self-fulfill the underlying prophecy and gain it back in order to be in alignment with what my Dark Voice was telling me. Nothing was going to change for me until I had a change of scenery from where and how I grew up.

There was no way I was going to be able to move on and start a new life within the same walls where I initially developed and currently lived my unhealthy coping mechanisms. For me, the swim team was going to be my first step in truly developing that stamina and commitment that would help me live on my own as a healthy person.

When I showed up for my tryout, I was completely intimidated by the fit, athletic bodies teeming in the water. Comparison at its best. Even though I felt okay in my suit, I couldn't lose focus on what I perceived to be my thunder thighs. In an attempt not to lose my nerve, I looked directly at the coach and pretended the perfect Merpeople weren't there.

I wasn't as fast as the other swimmers, but my stamina kicked in the moment I entered water. The underlying reason I was able to last as long and go as hard during that practice as those trained athletes was a high level of commitment. Commitment was a plus that developed in me over years of consistent application of the binge-and-sprint principles into my life. Yup, I sure knew how to work. Commitment creates stamina in any and all endeavors. It worked for me in the pool, but not for the right reasons (I wanted to be skinny). But when you drop your self-punishing reasons for hard work, and come to peace with your stamina and commitment, and allow it to be guided by healthy values or faith, you will get to wherever you want to go while also being your healthiest physical self. The goal is to see yourself as worthy as those around you, and for that commitment to serve your own soul that G-d went through the trouble of placing on this earth.

Throughout the Bible, the Jews are referred to as *Am k'shea oref,* which literally translates as "a thick-necked Nation," and is understood to mean "a stubborn people" or a people who don't give up. The swim team was going to teach me to take that skill set to an entirely new level and have it blossom into a different tool to assist me with a lifelong battle.

Practices lasted for two hours, five days a week, and twice daily on Mondays and Wednesdays. I was in heaven. I couldn't even imagine how many calories that would burn. I wasn't a sprinter in the pool, so I was swimming distance races, which burned even more calories. I felt like I had just won the skinny lottery. Beautiful body, here I come!

I was in pretty good shape at that time, and I started getting more comfortable with my body. But while I was running around the schoolyard with Annie playing X-Cookies and eating a whole box of cereal every Wednesday, these lean, muscular girls on the swim team had been athletes since they could walk. How on earth I thought I could look like them after just a few months of swimming is beyond me. Their legs were toned, while my thighs seemed to shake uncontrollably when I walked out onto the pool deck. My teammates and I even gave my oversized inner thighs a nickname: "jibbies." Now mind you, they didn't mean it as an insult; it was more a standard by which we all measured our jiggle. Although from my perspective, my jibbies clearly had the most jiggle. Their shoulders had so much definition during push-ups, and I didn't have any. While I waited on the bench for our events to be called, I noticed that their tummies were as flat as the kickboards we used during practice while mine always had a bulge no matter how little I ate or how many sit-ups I did. I wanted to look like them *right now*. I compared myself to those girls in an unhealthy way, and it wore on me every day. I had an expectation to reach a goal in an unreasonable amount of time while being in denial that I could ever look like someone I am not.

Comparison is a killer, and it robs you of loving your unique self. It conforms you to everyone else that you think is beautiful. It masks the magnificence of your personal spirit and your overall potential for success. It is the gateway drug for the Dark Voice to swoop in and tell you more compounding lies, like what you desire is not possible because of your failure to make the grade. Comparison puts on blinders so you don't see the Dark Voice coming. You can no longer acknowledge in a healthy way that if you've gotten this far, then you are more than capable of going all the way.

When I'm not yet in a state where I'm able to see others as

healthy inspiration for my own unique self, I crawl into a hole and stop trying, thinking in my heart of hearts that I can't rise to the occasion, and even if I did, it's way too scary to even try. Are you in the hole with me? Or are you obsessed with your mission and beating yourself up for not being perfect. Shall we tango together back and forth for a while?

How tired are we of this dance?

I would strive and strive and not reward myself for my efforts. I didn't experience joy in the process. I didn't give myself a break, a high-five, or a pat on the back, as that's not the binge-and-sprint way. I became driven like a machine toward an unrealistic goal that I would never attain because I was looking at myself through a distorted lens. I would work, but not experience the joy that the results brought. And if I did find joy, then I was out of alignment with the Dark Voice, and so those results must be obliterated and self-sabotaged until the results were no more. It was only after I had undone all that I worked so hard to achieve that I would allow myself to begin again, and round and round I'd go. Stamina and comparison were in a duel. I know what it's like to be stuck in both of these loops from hell.

One of our first swim meets was against New York University, and walking onto the pool deck was an experience within itself. Aside from the on-deck seating, there was bleacher seating and an overhead box viewing on top of that. It was a full twenty-five-meter pool with eight lap lanes. The venue was enormous and there were about three hundred people watching from all angles. NYU was a serious, competitive school, and it became increasingly clear as the meet progressed that we were going to get absolutely slaughtered. How we were even in the same division as they were was beyond me. I'm telling you, the NYU girls were like flying fish, and we were not even in the same league.

My event was the Four Hundred Meter Freestyle. I and two

other swimmers from Brooklyn College competed against three mermaids from NYU, so six lanes in total. I tucked all my hair under my cap, secured my goggles, and mounted the diving block.

My heart was racing out of my chest.

"Get set!"

I wrapped the ends of my toes and fingers around the edge of the block and said a prayer to the almighty swimming gods.

The gun went off.

I dove out as far as I could. I held my breath and swam underwater until I thought I would turn blue. As I approached the wall, I focused on my breathing so I would time it perfectly with my first flip turn. I executed, stretched my body as far as it would go, found a rhythm for the next thirty-eight flip turns and nineteen full laps, and settled in for the long haul.

My strokes and breathing effortlessly synced with my increasing heartbeat as the vision of my ultimate fantasy self played like a movie in my imagination. Driven like a locomotive, I could practically feel the calories melting off as I raced toward the person I was meant to be. It was definitely my fastest time yet.

My lap counter had already placed the cards in the water when I looked up. Eighteen. I had two more laps to go. I completed my flip turn and ricocheted off the wall. For the first time, I became cognizant of the swimmers in their lanes on either side of me. They were both a mere meter or two ahead of me, which was a miracle considering how fast they were in all the other races. My lap counter replaced the eighteen with nineteen as I approached the wall, and my heart nearly beat out of my chest with inordinate pride at the pace I was keeping. It was my personal best time! I quickly devised a plan to shorten the gap and maybe even tie or pull ahead of the other swimmers. Surely, it could be done with only one full lap left. In my mind's eye, I was already celebrating in the joyous rapture of victory that would certainly be mine. I felt myself getting closer to the person I was intended to be. I was so happy I could cry.

But as I approached the wall, with one full lap to go, the two swimmers on either side of me suddenly stopped at the end of their lanes.

Stopped? What's going on? Is there an emergency? Was someone threatening to drop a live hairdryer in the water? Did one of the swimmers poop? What on earth was so important that it would be the destruction of my one shot at greatness? Panicked, I whirled my head left and then right. I was only midway down the lane, so my vantage point from that angle was spot on. All of the swimmers had stopped at the wall. All of them! *Come on, Universe. I'm so close. Work with me here!*

It was then that I saw it.

My lap number said nineteen. But everyone else's said twenty. Everyone had lapped me. Everyone.

Six hundred eyes watched me from all angles. The ultimate humiliation.

My heart dropped into my stomach. The sensation of heat and pressure rising in my cheeks, my chest, my throat, and my head were overwhelming as I sucked back my tears. I was more devastated and demeaned in that moment than I had been in a long time. The evidence was clear. I was not fast enough no matter how I tried, and in correlation, not thin enough.

I had two choices. I could either touch the wall, put my feet down, and leave the pool with everyone else, hoping none of the onlookers would realize that I didn't complete the event. This option would perhaps save face, but it would also disqualify me from the event, which would subtract several points from my team, adding to their already increasing deficit against NYU. Or I could complete the event, which in reality was a lot worse than it sounded for two reasons. Number one, nobody was allowed to leave the pool until I finished. All the swimmers would have to stand there getting raisin toes as they watched and waited for me to finish. Number two, it wasn't proper etiquette to applaud until all swimmers had completed the event. That meant that all three hundred spectators had to sit in complete silence, listening to me splash as I stroked and kicked and turned. All three hundred spectators waiting and watching me from all angles.

I wanted more than anything to bolt and run from that pool, to the safety of the bench and huddle with my teammates. They would understand. They loved me and would never allow me to bear the burden of such shame. But I couldn't do it. I couldn't let my team down. Getting out of the pool went against the very grain and fiber of my being. In that moment, another asset bloomed. Uber commitment, stamina on steroids . . . or grit.

Grit was an indispensable quality that blossomed for me in that moment. I found myself laughing as I made that last lap. The comparison had taken a new form. Although I wouldn't understand the ultimate value of grit until decades later, I now know that it shaped my ability to eventually see whatever I'm going through from a place of self-love and acceptance.

When I look back at that moment, I realize that the very same excruciating challenges and burdens I had to bear throughout my life resulted in my ability to persist courageously in the face of my darkest fears and my deepest doubts. No matter how difficult it was to make that decision to swim that last lap, I didn't even really have to think about it. What I had to do was never a question in my mind. Even though I didn't have self-worth and the Dark Voice in my head ran rampant, I had grit, and I had integrity. And that felt good. Really good.

Well, at least it will be fifty more meters of calorie-burning exercise! I reasoned.

I finished that race! I straightened my arms over my head

and shook my fists in victory. The crowd erupted with applause. I jumped up on the pool deck and was immediately swept up by my teammates in a massive hug as they laughed with me, not at me. I faced that situation with my new friend Grit. Not forced grit, not driving, punishing grit, but a true appreciation for what I accomplished. I was proud of myself for not letting everyone down. But more importantly, I was able to laugh about the situation instead of caring what others thought of me or comparing myself to the other swimmers. In that moment, the loyalty and dependability I had demonstrated to my team overrode my personal Dark Voice that told me I should be embarrassed and that I wasn't enough. This new awareness of my self-worth was determined by using grit to overcome challenges, and I came out the other side the better for it. But that awareness didn't happen overnight. It took decades of careful and frequent application to acknowledge my self-worth.

This was a massive step up from the little girl who ate the cereal for the benefit of her family. For the good of my swim team, I let go of some of my doubt about my worth. I proved to myself that I could finish what I started no matter how difficult, and I developed my character for the better in the process. That's the exact arsenal I needed in my war with food. When stretching myself for the benefit of others, I replaced taking from myself with giving something to me. And that was a massive step in the direction of squashing the Dark Voice.

There is a Jewish saying that "G-d sends the *refuah* [healing] before the *macah* [plague]," meaning that he provides within each of us the means to learn and recognize the solution for the challenges we encounter. I was beginning to use the tools I gained from binge and sprint as a force for good, which would eventually allow me the strength to free myself from the Dark Voice forever.

Would I now begin to think of myself as worthy? Absolutely

not. Every swimmer had lapped me! But the experience had more depth and weight down the road when all the decades of binge and sprint had trapped me and I couldn't see a way out. I relied on an experience such as the swim meet as proof of my stamina and grit and that I could rise again, with new life and knowledge of who I was becoming.

I learned from that swim meet that when you immerse yourself in the uncomfortable, the scary, and the unfamiliar, it opens the door for you to be uplifted beyond what kept you from approaching those opportunities in the first place. Yes, I joined the swim team to get skinny. I wanted to be skinny so badly that I joined even though tons of spectators would see my jibbies. I did it because I thought I would find my self-worth in a skinny body. And however misguided that was, it put me in a position to experience finding my self-worth through something completely unexpected and so much more meaningful.

In order to have a transcendental experience, you need to first expose yourself to the challenges or you can never transcend them. So how can you expose yourself to risks and discomforts that bring the big rewards? No matter how hard, how long the road, how painful, how scary, how arduous the task, you must always, *always* finish your race. As Winston Churchill said, "Never give in, never give in, never, never, never." Weight loss and being skinny was my ultimate race and would continue to be, but I was also developing new aspects of myself for when I came into who I was destined to truly be down the road of life. Even if you don't understand why you are having an all-out battle in your head with a toasted everything bagel smothered in melted butter while your sister is happy to pick at a salad, you must trust and have faith that the truth will reveal itself in just the right time. Keep going, and do not give up under any circumstance. No matter how many times you need to snap yourself out of the comparison game, whether they see you fail, or how great your embarrassment, just remember that it's your race, not theirs. So make it great.

CHAPTER 4

Summer

As the saying goes: "If I could have bought myself for what I thought I was worth, and then turned around and sold myself for what I was actually worth, I would have made millions." I wasn't able to see myself for who I truly was. Even if I reached my goal weight, or was the most beautiful girl in the world, or became my ideal physical self in every way and didn't binge as much as I did, I was always peeking into a distorted mirror instead of into the depths of my soul. I was on the same radio frequency with the Dark Voice and couldn't find G-d's station on the dial. No matter what I achieved, I could never be that perfect girl I hoped to be. She was always a grasp away.

But she had a name. Summer.

I created Summer in sleep-away camp. Every year, from the ages of seven to seventeen, my sisters and I were shipped off to the Catskills like all the other good Jewish children from respectable New York homes. My parents worked really hard to give us that gift, and I will be grateful for it all the days of my life. Those were innocent, carefree days with no fighting or yelling, no demands to rush about and be constructive, and fun and laughter were the name of the game. I made my best friends and my best memories during those precious weeks. And because my anxiety and responsibility levels were at an all-time low, I always returned home at least ten pounds lighter, on occasion an inch taller, and consistently with a radiant complexion. I returned home the vision of Summer. She was all sunshine, light, and warmth.

Summer looked exactly like me, but her hair was extra long and bouncy and shiny, glistening in the sunlight like that girl in the Breck Shampoo commercial. Her skin was sun-kissed, glowing, and radiant, as if it were the collective presumption of her sebaceous glands that she was just too perfect to be subjected to any and all forms of blemish. Her teeth were aligned flawlessly in a broad, pearly-white smile that illuminated her entire presence. And although she was me, she appeared much taller than my five-two frame and of course slimmer. And more muscular. And prettier. She wore a white T-shirt tucked into white jean shorts, and her thighs didn't touch when she walked. They didn't so much as shake one bit as she elegantly bounded across the street to her destination, and she certainly did not have jibbies.

There was always an element of excited surprise with Summer where the days weren't planned and scheduled, and the rules and regulations were relaxed. She embodied the anticipation I felt toward those endless summer days where anything could happen, where everything was possible.

I used Summer as a visualization tool to stop myself from stuffing my face. I lacked personal insight or therapy to explain to me that I binged due to a lot of *mishegas* (Yiddish for "crazy nonsense") from unresolved family trauma, so I employed my own strategies. I had wars in my head that sounded like, *I'm not going to eat that, but it looks so good. What if I just have one? No, I said I wouldn't. But if I trade all my starches for the day for this one brownie* . . . So in stepped Summer visualizations.

Visualization, the process of creating a mental picture of the achievement of your goals, is now recommended by all of these fabulous, high-performance coaches and law of attraction people. I didn't know all of this back then. I was just doing it to keep myself from eating an entire fresh-baked challah by myself. I leaned into what it would feel like to be Summer, and I let this feeling take over me, which would sustain me until the next time that I was presented with a platter of chocolate chip cookies. Visualization worked really well, but the problem was that Summer didn't win every battle. I gave in to the extra food when the chips were down, and I lost grasp of the good Summer feeling. Even though Summer was a massive motivator as a construct, she wasn't getting to the emotional root of my turmoil. But when I was able to hold the Summer visualization, and feeling her as me, all forms of cake crossed my radar with much less frequency. I was able to focus on this ideal self and act in accordance with what would take me there. I did not fully understand how brilliant this tool was until years later when it all started to come together that I had to commit to a good life permanently. No more ups and downs. But from my college years until I turned fifty, I would use the "Summer method" sporadically and, consequently, I would go up and down in weight for another thirty years.

Then the ultimate mind-blowing day came. Have you ever had that aha moment where something just clicks? Your life may not change forever right then and there, but you know you will never be the same because a massive seed was planted in your psyche. Well, get this . . . I actually met Summer! My first job out of college was at Turner Broadcasting where I was a sales administrative assistant, a.k.a. secretary. I made it a habit to stay just a little bit later than necessary, and it was dark outside when I left. As is usual for the City That Never Sleeps, all the streetlights were on and I hustled through the throngs of business people and tourists to catch the express bus home. The light turned green and I jolted across Fifth Avenue.

Then I saw her. I couldn't believe it.

It was Summer.

I saw the girl in the white shorts in my brain, now donning a long black coat, right behind me in the reflection of the building across the street. I almost froze in the middle of Fifth Avenue. I watched her in the reflection of the mirrored building as she floated elegantly across the street, her body slim and perfectly in proportion, her hair shimmering in the streetlights, bouncing in perfect unison with her steps. She was the most beautiful woman I had ever seen, and she took my breath away. Her mere image had a visceral effect on me. I felt my resolve rising. I heard the words in my head that I would work even harder to become the person I always wanted to be. That I deserved to look and feel beautiful and I would make it happen. I would pump up my exercise routine and cut down on the food even more. And then I felt inferior to this woman, comparing myself and doubting that I would ever look and feel the way I wanted. Even though I had accomplished so much and had begun to receive consistent external approval, I still couldn't see it in myself. My self-worth dropped into the toilet. My heart sank.

As I reached the curb I saw my express bus approaching, and I raised my hand to signal to the familiar driver who brought me home every day. And then the strangest thing happened. Summer raised her hand too. I turned to see if she would be getting on my bus, and her reflection that I was watching in the mirrored building turned too.

I looked back to my reflection only to find that Summer, the beautiful girl in my head in the white shorts in the black coat, was me.

I stood there in disbelief, my mouth agape, paralyzed and

cemented to my spot on the sidewalk, staring at my reflection in the mirrored facade of the building as New Yorkers pushed and shoved and sped by. My bus driver honked impatiently. I just stood there. For the first time I saw myself through the eyes of a stranger and through the eyes of G-d: perfect and whole. I was hit with the magnitude of the disparity between how I had seen myself for my whole life and my current reality. The sound of the express bus driver shutting the doors snapped me out of my trance and I turned and bolted onto the bus.

I'll never forget that ride home. I thought a lot about Summer and how I had been obsessed with becoming her. She was my ideal of what complete confidence looked like, and I strove with all my might to attain what she had, but I had set myself up for failure from the start. Looking back, I don't know what I was thinking. The girl in my head had a thigh gap. Dear reader, I could be a size zero and my thighs will still touch when I walk. I just have those thighs. Come to think of it, the white-shorts girl in my brain didn't have my body type at all. She was long and lean, and I'm short and square. I'll never even reach five-three in this lifetime. Summer was built like a swimmer or a runner or a ballet dancer, and I'm more the diver, fit-looking type when I'm at my best. I had set an impossible standard to reach, and I'm not clear as to why I would do that to myself. Was it the Dark Voice tricking me so that I would stay forever lacking in self-worth, completely malleable and subservient under his rule? Or was it my own psyche telling me that I needed to become a different person altogether? And if that was the case, that needed to stop. G-d Himself made me, and I was perfect in his eyes. I just needed to find out how to make right what I thought was damaged goods.

Oscar Wilde said, "To love oneself is the beginning of a lifelong romance." I'm not saying that after meeting Summer, and understanding that I already was her, that I was suddenly never hard on myself or beat myself up for no reason, or stopped doubting my abilities. All of that was still pretty much intact, but a seed had been planted. The Dark Voice was part of my human experience, and I'll have those shadows lurking in the background my whole life. But a glimmer of liberation was planted. I saw for myself the beauty and worth within me through the eyes of strangers, although maybe not through my own eyes just yet.

My husband, Alex, saw me as beautiful way before I could even think of myself that way. He is gorgeous, my husband, truly. I don't know how I got so lucky, but kindred spirits find each other like we did in New York City that night at a party for Jewish singles. I was still hot on the working out and weighing and measuring my food trail. I was wearing a fitted blazer with massive shoulder pads, tall black boots, opaque tights, and a denim Guess mini skirt that came to my mid-thigh with a zipper up the back (I still have that skirt, and my daughters recently tried to "liberate" it from my closet). It's so funny that I remember two things about the memorable events in my life: what I was wearing, and how much I weighed.

I saw him across the room—tall, with a head of wavy light-brown rock star hair, and blue-green eyes, with the bone structure of a classic movie star and a physique to match. He wore a turtleneck and a black leather jacket with straight-legged jeans covering his boots and mile-long legs. It was as if I were momentarily glued to the floor and rendered completely immobile. I couldn't get enough air into my lungs as he passed right by me to his friends sitting at the bar. He didn't even notice me or look my way.

Oh well, I thought to myself. *Completely out of my league.*

The party was almost over, and Melissa and I were heading out when we were stopped by a guy who was clearly interested in her. In an attempt to keep me occupied, he called over a wingman. Can you guess who it was? Mr. Gorgeous himself! I don't know if he knew I had been following him around all night trying to get him to notice me to no avail . . . but there he was. Smiling down at me. And it was a real smile, the smile of someone who was actually interested in meeting me.

"Hi," I gushed as I involuntarily lit up like Times Square at midnight.

And what came next was the most unexpected, thrilling thing I have ever heard in my life.

"You are the most beautiful girl I have ever seen, and I've been following you around all night," Alex said.

Needless to say, I gave him my number.

Our first date was at a cozy bar called Brew's on East Thirty-Fourth Street. "I don't understand," I said. "How is it possible that you are so gorgeous and so nice?"

"Oh," he answered with a chuckle. "I used to be fat."

Stop it!

"No way! Me too!" I offered without even feeling worried about the repercussions of admitting that because of how safe and accepted he made me feel.

His eyes widened. "No, you're so beautiful. It's not possible. I don't believe that."

On and on it went, through our war stories and common understanding.

It all started when Alex was a teenager. He and his posse intervened to save a friend from a group of bullies, and the situation was saved when Alex entered the scene. This earned him his nickname that would stick with him over the long haul, and which he had a hand in inventing due to what he perceived to be his most valuable asset at the time: Ox. And therein lies the difference between growing up overweight as a boy and growing up overweight as a girl. I always felt people determined that I was not as pretty or worthy because I was overweight. But boys are put in a different stereotype altogether. You can't call someone who identifies as a girl "Ox" by any stretch of the imagination without it being hurtful. A name like Ox is specifically for a male, and plays two sides of the same coin. At best, an ox can move heavy things or situations out of the way. An ox gets things done with sheer brute force and commands respect for it. Nobody in their right mind wants to mess with the ox.

But if a young man aspires to be anything more than a farm animal that pushes things out of their way despite their size, it can be difficult to lose that identity. Everyone knew Alex as Ox, but he yearned to be something different. Perhaps a gazelle that swiftly wins in the race of life, or a fox that can out-think his opponents, or an eagle that spreads his wings and soars to limitless potential. But he was labeled as an ox, a bully who took what he wanted and just lumbered along. He felt like Moose Mason from the *Archie* comics. A lumbering oaf.

My heart bled for him, and I felt akin to him. I wondered if he perceived me as I perceived him. As this perfect, beautiful, fit being who came out of nowhere without the bias of him knowing my former self. Yet there we were, embracing each other's past and faults and measures of worth.

We were so mesmerized by each other and immersed in each other's presence that we didn't even notice the time, or that the bar owners had swept up, locked up, cleaned up, and put the chairs up on the tables. One of them cleared their throat, and we looked up to find the owners lined up by the bar, looking at us with huge grins on their faces. Clearly, they didn't want to interrupt the blooming of young love for as long as possible, but it was time to get going. Alex held my hand through the deserted streets as he walked me back to my friend's dorm where I was staying for the night. And as I watched him go on his way, I knew I would marry him. I just knew. I floated to the elevator and snuck into my friend's dorm room where she and her roommates were already fast asleep. I got under the blankets on the mattress on the floor she had set up for me as quietly as I could, eager to review the night's events in my mind.

I was Summer and Summer was me in that moment. We had melded.

But almost as soon as I got comfortable relishing in the miracle that had just happened that would change the trajectory of my life for the better forever, I was gripped with panic and fear. *What if it's not real?* I thought. *What if someone put him up to all of this? What if it's a joke?*

In the blink of an eye, I was overcome by the terror spewed by the Dark Voice. I couldn't fully wrap my brain around being worthy of so much unconditional love, unearned adoration, and life-altering warmth and kindness. I tossed and turned and cried all night, unable to let go of the terror that the sheer, unbridled joy I had just so intensely experienced could be ripped away from me because it was never even real to begin with. I didn't understand it then, but in my heart I couldn't believe I was worthy of something so wonderful. I was being terrorized by an oppressor that existed only in my mind. I was still living in my parents' house, so I had not shifted fully into the belief that I could have another reality. My own home and existence, something that Naomi created, one that was buried deep by so many years of conditioning that I honestly didn't even know it was possible. I didn't know why I felt so bad and was therefore completely at the mercy of my unconscious responses and the emotions they produced. How could I have stood up and eradicated a prison that I didn't even understand I was in? I was completely unaware of the toll of so many years of binge and sprint. The Dark Voice had made me feel unworthy, not good enough, undeserving, and overweight. The consistent demeaning condescension of the Dark Voice burdened me for years to come.

But the Dark Voice doesn't rule the world. G-d does, and Alex stayed around. He became my rock.

He helped me to see clearly and resolve the issues that prompted me to go into fight or flight. He took control of the wheel when I couldn't, and then handed it to me when I was ready. He protected me by seeing through a different set of eyes and finding resolutions where I didn't know one could even exist. And he was kind. Kinder than I knew it was possible for one person to be to another. We all need people in our lives who are our champions. Who love us no matter what and understand our struggles.

Who do you reach out to for unconditional love? Who accepts you despite the mess of your own binge and sprint?

Our courtship was full of everything I dreamed it would be, and surprises I never expected. We got engaged eighteen months later on a perfect night in early September, two weeks before the Jewish High Holy Days.

I was sitting with my mother in synagogue that Yom Kippur when the Dark Voice returned. My life looked perfect, and I guess the Dark Voice thought so too. I was going to marry the man of my dreams. I had a fabulous new studio in the perfect location, and a new job at a small specialty firm as a full-blown advertising sales executive. Alex was applying to law school. I was thin and fit, looked beautiful in clothing, and worked out regularly. It was all going so well, and I couldn't shake the absolute terror that one of those things would be taken away from me. The anxiety of it all was killing me, and I bawled my eyes out on that Day of Atonement in synagogue. The prayers of the day could not more perfectly reflect the uncertainty with which I faced the coming year.

"On Yom Kippur will be sealed . . . Who will rest and who will wander, who will live in harmony and who will be harried, who will enjoy tranquility and who will suffer, who will be impoverished and who will be enriched, who will be degraded and who will be exalted."

Even though that prayer ended with a resounding promise that repentance, prayer, and charity would remove the evil of the decree, I wasn't convinced that what I had to offer would be enough. My life lay in the hands of G-d. My G-d, the One who I served and trusted and loved and prayed to daily all my life. Yet the Dark Voice made me doubt my safety, even under the wing of the Almighty. I truly did not know if G-d would find me worthy of all the good coming my way, or if I was strong enough to fight off the Dark Voice when it beckoned me away from the light. I wanted the life of my dreams, but at the same time I couldn't imagine living it. I didn't yet believe that untethered joy was my intended lot in life, no matter the strength of my faith.

And so I prayed with all my heart to find my faith. To this day, I don't remember ever praying with a more powerful, sincere connection, or what we call in Hebrew, *kavanah.*

I beseeched G-d to watch over me that year. But what I was really praying for was the strength to give my intended life to myself. G-d had already opened His hand to me—I am now certain of that to the fiber of my very being. But what I couldn't count on was that I would defy the Dark Voice and make the choice to give it to myself. It wasn't that I was afraid G-d would take something away from me. I was afraid that I would take it from me.

I was so convinced and so accustomed to the belief system I had developed over my life that only work was for me, not the beauty and joy that came with the culmination of that work. I wish I could say that I overcame and fully claimed my birthright right then and there, but I didn't. The next decades of my life would be filled with me carrying out the wishes of the Dark Voice and closing my own hand to myself, although I didn't recognize it as such at the time.

When I picture myself standing in synagogue that day, I'm now reminded of the key to our home that we bake into our challah bread for the first Sabbath after Passover every year. The baking of *shlissel* (Yiddish for *key*) challah is a tradition that is looked forward to every year. We bake a key into the challah bread as a symbol of our hope that G-d will unlock the gates of sustenance and abundance into our lives. There is a prayer that accompanies the making of *shlissel* challah where we site one hundred gates that we pray will be opened for us. The gates of being saved, the gates of charity, the gates of joy, the gates of getting up and moving forward, the gates of piety, the gates of a full recovery, the gates of a good life, the gates of wisdom, the gates of song, the gates of redemption, the gates of long life, the gates of blessing, the gates of love, and eighty-seven other wonderful things.

Looking back, I realize with a heavy heart that I wasn't praying that G-d would give me the key. I already had it. I was praying I would be strong enough to realize my deserving and use that key to turn open the locks. And even though the sad truth is that I didn't use that key to open all the gates I had kept shut to myself for many more years, it was my faith that I found through prayer that day that gave me enough strength to begin moving forward. When the fast was finally over and I left the synagogue, I used that faith and my trust in Alex to help me work through my fear. Alex could make me feel safe anywhere.

CHAPTER 5

Public Eating

I've spent a lifetime shaping my environment to make it easy to reach for healthy food, instead of fixing my relationship with food to guarantee healthy eating habits in all environments. I would meticulously put into place every strategy known to man that I'd learned from years of trial and error around my current schedule, living arrangement, responsibilities, and who I shared a common space with until I could get through my day of food in a healthy way without a hitch. I never thought for one minute to stop and ask, "Who is Naomi with food?" If I had allowed myself to slow down from sprinting for long enough to make that identification, cement it into my brain, and live the part, it would have helped in not allowing anyone or anything to derail me from the knowing and living of my true self. But did I do that? Nope. I would just cruise along, taking life's little speed bumps until there was a more radical life change and I'd end up with a complete food implosion.

I didn't know how to have a healthy relationship with food, eating, hunger, being satisfied, and fullness. I'd find the rug pulled out from under me from erratic food habits. Down I would fall into the eating abyss until I finally found enough strength and familiarity within my new environment to crawl back out and set it up all over again, which could take years. That was clearly not the best strategy. I needed to get my relationship with food effortless and organic, aligning with its true nature and highest purpose for my ultimate good no matter the surroundings, otherwise everything gets willy-nilly with the flip of life's every switch.

Being married had affected my relationship with food. Alex's relationship to food was the opposite of mine. He ate different foods, at different times, and even the portion size was not the same. He's from Argentina, the land of afternoon siestas and midnight steak dinners. I clearly remember my utter confusion when his family in Maryland sat down to a full-on meal, with dessert, after a late-night movie. Although we were both Orthodox Jews, culturally our eating habits were learned and nurtured in different stratospheres.

For the two years prior to our nuptials, I was living in my own Upper West Side apartment in Manhattan. I was in a completely independent food-prep space, which I falsely identified as a permanent liberty from bingeing. I truly believed that the Dark Voice and out-of-control eating I'd been doing forever would simply die off because I was no longer under my parents' roof. Nothing could be further from the truth. I had not yet developed a reliable identification with food that would automatically keep my eating steady. My method *du jour* holding me to my ideal weight was a rigid, structured daily diet and exercise plan from my college days bumped up a notch . . . or two. But surprisingly, this structure allowed me to catch a glimpse of what relaxing with food could eventually look like. Because my life was dominated by a structured meal and exercise plan, there was temporarily no need for the food wars to continue in my head, and I actually had time to be quiet and think, and I daresay *feel* what my body wanted. A temporary foray into what it would be like to have an actual beneficial relationship with food.

Structure was a perfect strategy for that time in my life, but it was fragile and temporary because it didn't get to the root of the bingeing. Structure on its own was just a Band-Aid holding together the issues of my childhood festering beneath. Yet at the same time, I was building a repertoire of skills I'd implement to one day create a routine that was happy and healthy for my body and soul. Just when I got the structure down nearly perfect, the Dark Voice and out-of-control eating hopped on the subway to Forest Hills, following me to my new marital abode.

"Do you really have to be that structured in giving your body healthy foods and regular exercise?" asked the Dark Voice.

"Heck yeah!" is my current answer as a fifty-three-year-old woman.

"Well, maybe. Kind of," was my answer as a newlywed who was eager to please and morph as one with her husband no matter his eating habits.

By the way, you don't have to be married by any means to pivot to someone else's eating habits. Here's a perfect example of what I'm talking about. Let's say you're dating someone who's in a band. You normally go to bed at a decent time to get up early so you can get to the gym before work, but he has gigs several nights a week playing at bars and weddings. Your date starts just before midnight because he has the freedom to sleep in until noon. You want to be the girl he adores, so you mess up your whole schedule to go and catch some of his set, after which the two of you rendezvous over late-night pizza or whatever the restaurant owner has left over because he's starving, and naturally you can't have him eating alone. You're exhausted the next day and don't get up to exercise or do whatever else feeds your soul in the morning. As a result, you're completely off-kilter, falling asleep at work, and your pants are getting tight. You start to resent the relationship, but you know if you simply say, "I can't live this way anymore," the relationship is shot dead in the water. And he isn't changing for you. He's a musician. That's the lifestyle, take it or leave it. So, you put on weight and tell yourself you are going to start working out after work instead of the morning, but that never happens. One day at work, you bend over to reach for a file and your pants split open down the middle. You realize that perhaps this lifestyle isn't for you, and you put that relationship down like a bad habit. You promise yourself you will be stricter next time with dating, with anyone, with everyone, and with all things threatening to take you away from being the best you, but the Dark Voice tells you that you won't get what you want if you are not flexible. So that up-and-down begins again. And once more, your alliance to your body's needs are pushed to the side while everyone else's needs are front and center.

Alex did not play in a band, nor did he make any demands on me that would be considered a sacrifice. I put them all on myself. I met Alex when I was smack dab in the middle of my zone of health. I had even seen myself as Summer, for goodness' sake! I was fit, working, and independent as I started living in my own space away from my parents only four months after we started dating. When we got married and moved in together, I just wanted to be a team player. To be carefree and have fun with all things including food. I thought, *How bad could eating poorly here and there really be?* But I didn't realize I was setting myself up on a tightrope, two stories in the air with no net by not owning how I needed to eat for my soul. Somewhere in the back of my head, the Dark Voice was whispering into my psyche that something could still be taken from me if I didn't become a chameleon and get myself in line with the current program. I didn't even realize it was happening until it was too late because I was so perfectly programmed over years of using the same mechanisms of doing what others expected me to do that I adjusted subconsciously and my actions automatically followed. The Dark Voice was so loud and ever present in my brain that quiet Naomi introspection was out the window along with structure. I was still powerless to stop running and appeasing everyone, and my body, my self-worth, and my soul took the hit.

There was another glitch in this whole married-living thing, one that I didn't think of until the first time I was putting away groceries in our kitchen. I ran the risk of being caught stuffing and overeating depending on how stealth I was in my bingeing and sprinting. Man, I was *really* hoping Alex wouldn't notice that I turned to food in my times of need. But as it turns out, I was in luck. Like all the other guys his age who recklessly filled their bottomless pits with abandon and never gained an ounce, my twenty-one-year-old husband ate crappy food late at night. There was nothing taboo about keeping Entenmann's in the house right there in the open, and no questions asked if an entire box went missing. This was a bizarre and strange new world, and I had no clue which end was up. Had I just hit the jackpot, or was I entering an alternate realm from which I would never return? Either way, it was unchartered territory, and unfortunately, I did not proceed with caution. I knew *nothing* about sticking to my guns regarding what I needed to properly nourish myself, as nothing trumped what I would do to keep Alex or anything of this new and wonderful life from going away. Clearly, Alex was not looking at what I put on my plate—that is, if what I was shoving into my mouth even made it onto a plate. I was the one not owning what type of eating didn't work for me. I was the one who couldn't stand up and say, "No, that's not for me. That doesn't work for me." The result was that I did not establish a new and peaceful way of eating in my new and peaceful marriage, and I would play catch-up for the next twenty-six years. Even though the eating differences between the two of us would eventually disappear, there would always be another reason I couldn't piece together a healthy eating regime for myself to replace the reason that came before that. My inability to set it up right from the get-go had nothing to do with Alex and his eating habits after all. It was me and my past conditioning. It was all me.

When we were first married, I remember coming home once in a flurry of activity. It was Sunday, and I had a long list of very specific errands to accomplish before returning to work the next morning. I unlocked the apartment door, carrying multiple bags from different stores. Alex was sitting on the couch.

"Hey, what are you doing?" I asked him.

"Nothing."

"Nothing?"

"Well, not nothing. I'm relaxing."

Okay, this was a new one for me. I paused like a deer in head-lights trying to wrap my brain around what he just said. I honestly had no idea what he was talking about.

"Yeah, but like, what are you doing to relax? Are you going to watch TV? Are you reading?"

"No. I'm just relaxing."

Mind melting. *No comprende.*

"Come here and try it. I'll show you."

"No!" I was grossly offended by the mere thought of it and made a horrible face like someone had just asked me to eat spiders.

"Come here, you'll like it," he said.

I really did not want to play this twisted game, but I was newly married and wanted to be a team player, and in a strange way I was intrigued by the thought that maybe he was onto something.

I put down my bags and went over to the couch.

"Okay, what do I do?" I asked skeptically.

"Okay." He was so excited to show me. "Sit down right here next to me."

"Okay. Now what?"

"Now get comfortable."

"Okay. I'm comfortable. Now what?"

"Now just relax."

"Okay, I'm relaxed. Now what?"

"Now just relax."

Five, four, three, two, one.

I jumped up.

"I don't like this! I'm not doing this!" I was beyond weirded out. I honestly did not know what kind of sick game he was playing, but I was not raised like that. *My G-d, who just sits on a couch relaxing smack in the middle of the day? And not even doing anything to relax? Insane!* It went against every fiber of my being. Seriously, my hair stood up on ends and I got the willies.

There is a Grand Canyon between binge and sprint and just relaxing. Maimonides, a medical doctor and one of the most prolific Jewish philosophers and scholars of the Middle Ages, said that when you are all the way on one side of something, you swing like a pendulum all the way to the other extreme. After swinging back and forth for a while—visiting both sides and experiencing them evenly—the swinging slows down and you are able to rest in the middle, peacefully and effortlessly incorporating both. The Dark Voice incorporating binge and sprint is one extreme side of the pendulum.

One of the rules of binge and sprint is that you always need to be busy or on a mission. Always sprinting toward something. Now, there is nothing wrong with using your time efficiently. It's actually something that I actively strive to master in my life. But here's the difference: with binge and sprint, weight is just another type of mission that you have to be busy with, and bingeing on food has all the qualifications of being busy. I carried this belief from when I was eight and ate the box of Cap'n Crunch because I was all alone for the first time in my house. It's a time-consuming activity where you are constantly moving, and therefore a binge-and-sprint staple. So, in the logical world of awareness, people use their time being busy with working toward what they want, like a healthy body. In the binge-and-sprint world, people get busy with the things the Dark Voice wants.

Here's what the Dark Voice says right before overeating: "What are you doing? Are you going to listen to me and believe that you're as thin as you deserve and it's time to gain weight now? Get busy shoving as much high-caloric food into your mouth, and get on with the doing of getting fat. You need this food to sprint to your next task, so get on with the bingeing! Move!"

If you've ever stood at the counter stuffing yourself with stale rice cakes shoved into jars of jelly that were opened before the flood, or stood in the opened fridge putting together other concoctions that are just as disgusting, you know what I mean. I'm sorry if that image is painful, but we have to get real and honest if we're going to fix it.

In order to get past overeating, you need to look within and at the core of your lifestyle, no matter your surroundings, and ask yourself how you are going to succeed within that to have the body you desire. Sure, if you just got married, or if your friends want you to go on a wine and chocolate weekend in Sonoma, you'll need good structure and good stamina to beat food . . . always. But first you have to love you more than anyone else.

I didn't see how I was passively submitting to others with eating in my faith, as Jews have a complicated relationship with food. It was in this area that I birthed the concept of "public bingeing". I did have some previous knowledge of public bingeing, although it wasn't as intimate as my frequent experience with private bingeing. But I soon became an expert in both categories because during the first seven years of our marriage living in Forest Hills—the mecca for young, married Modern Orthodox Jewish couples—we ate with other people . . . all the time.

During the week, food is supposed to be viewed simply as fuel for our bodies so we can carry out G-d's commandments and go about our daily lives. The Berditcheva Rebbe was famous for speaking about and doing just that. But he also said that special, beautifully prepared foods are meant to make Sabbath more beautiful and special as well.

In our common apartment hallways on Thursday nights, smells from the kitchens of Jewish newlyweds of homemade challah bread, rich meats, kugels of all sorts, chicken soup, roasting vegetables, and rich desserts baking hung in the air. Decadent, expensive foods prepared with special care are meant to sanctify Sabbath, and we further sanctify the food by making blessings over it and taking pleasure in it. (Note how I said "special" foods, not "fattening" foods. Fattening is not part of the criteria, although it's certainly part of the experience.) The more pleasure you get from it, the more you are appreciating Sabbath and making it holy. Maimonides wrote an entire book, which is available today, on how to eat properly for the healthiest bodies we can possibly have. And I'm pretty sure he doesn't tell you to incorporate muffins and a latte as part of your daily breakfast. It is a common old wives' tale, or what is known in Yiddish as a *bubbah meisa,* that you should eat to your heart's content on Sabbath because your body can't gain weight on this holy day. Puh-leeze. Go to any nutritionist or diet center in any Jewish neighborhood and the staff there will easily be able to document otherwise. Just the challah alone can single-handedly wipe out an entire week of careful diet and exercise. My goodness, how did we ever get so far from the soul-lifting sanctification food was intended to be? From how food was meant to serve us instead of ruling over us? How did any of us get so far from the people we are supposed to be in the bodies we are supposed to be in?

And the food doesn't end when Sabbath does. Saturday night was meant for group trips to the movies or bowling, and then we would all pile into someone's apartment for pizza and ice cream. So there I was, public bingeing freely and in full view of others in social situations. This is different from private bingeing, which is done in solitude, often in the dark of the kitchen, alone, hoping you won't be caught, hyper listening for any and all approaching humans. You can equally shame yourself for both, but public bingeing feels more celebratory. That is, until you can't zip your jeans. The same food wars are going on in your head in full force during both public and private bingeing. In public binging, there's also a lot of peer pressure to participate in conversation about the food, and generally be socially aware of the food. For example, if the person on your right is talking about how delicious the chocolate cake is, and the person on your left is discussing the perfect consistency of the chocolate chip cookies, then by G-d, clearly you need to eat both in order to fully participate in both conversations! Additionally, there are obvious complicating factors when you are sitting at a table in front of food for hours. At some point, you eat the decadence in front of you to either fill the time, keep yourself stimulated to stay awake, or just start popping small cookies into your mouth as a mindless yet tasty activity.

Private and public bingeing can at times have a common denominator of being linked to anxious feelings, but they serve a very different purpose. While you may publicly binge to satiate social transitioning, private bingeing assists you in transitioning from one feeling or activity to another, and these activities are usually harder tasks you feel insecure about or having difficulty leaning into. With public bingeing, you get to eat the foods of your dreams, unlike private binges where you're oftentimes cowering in the kitchen eating who-knows-what leftover garbage. This may lead you to believe that public bingeing is superior to private bingeing, but you'd be wrong. The benefit to private bingeing is relief from transitioning from one state of being to another, and most times, there is no food that tastes as sweet as getting to the other side. But no matter how you slice it (again with the puns), you feel the same awful way after it's over. You're in a gluten fog, your clothes feel tight, you're uncomfortably bloated, you're beyond sorry you did it, and you promise yourself you'll never do it again. Another notch in the belt of the Dark Voice, and another peg lower on the measuring stick of your self-worth for not putting your own needs first.

And just when you think that you at least have the food some-what handled despite all the private and public bingeing, life gets busier, more hectic, more real. From this point in my life, I didn't stop sprinting for a long time. All at once I was working a full-time job, putting Alex through law school, taking prerequisites, and applying to graduate school to be a speech therapist. On weekends, I actively played the role of the consummate entertainer, and I threw in teaching aerobics classes at the local gym on top of that just for kicks. I began with a sprint, chasing my future of endless possibilities of what a master's degree would bring my way with all the exuberance in my heart. While there was so much of my authentic joy wrapped up in that undertaking, deep down there was still a void I was trying to fill. Who was I deep in my soul? I still needed that external approval and was looking out when I should have been filling myself up from within. That little girl who lived inside of me, who still didn't believe she was enough, so desperately needed validation. To be loved, to be cherished should be a rite of passage, but sometimes the path gets winding and we lose our way. We begin to believe that we need to prove our worth by being thin, or accomplished, or getting a master's degree, or having a baby, and we certainly don't wait around for what we want. That is lazy! What are you doing that's constructive to get you to where you want to go? What did you do to improve yourself lately? You have to always be going for something in order to be worthy! And so I continued the sprint.

To top it all off, I discovered a big, huge fibroid that needed to be surgically removed if we ever wanted to have children. After my surgery, I couldn't exercise for a while, and then conveniently fell out of the routine as I busied myself making dinners and purchasing gifts for all of my friends' new babies that arrived at synagogue each week. At the same time, I discovered a new passion within my studies. As it turns out, one integral element in the study of Speech and Language Pathology is feeding and swallowing disorders. How cool was that? Feeding and swallowing! I was already an expert in that, and I took to the classes and the subsequent work in the both the clinic and beyond like a fish to water. I felt completely at home assisting patients in this area, and it became one of my specialties for the duration of my career.

With a newly illuminated career path, I rationalized that I couldn't spare the time to exercise. Additionally, I found myself studying alone at home much of the time. As I was buried under work, projects were regularly put off until the last minute, and studying for tests became huge, looming monsters that were incredibly scary to approach. This overwhelming, anxiety-ridden feeling that I wouldn't do perfectly on my exams, proving that I was not enough, led to a semester-long private binge in the form of boxes of graham crackers dipped in Skippy smooth peanut butter. I knew I should have been hitting the books, but I couldn't get the graham crackers out of my head. Just the thought of them in the cupboard drove me wild. They knew just how to satisfy me.

I tried to keep my focus on my assignments, but their delicious pull was more than I could resist. At first it was fun—a secret I kept all to myself—but before long, our time together was making me uncomfortable. My pants were getting tight, and I couldn't focus on my upcoming exams. But I couldn't stop. That's when I made the call to my best friend, Dani. She lived right across the street. I could tell her anything, and I knew she wouldn't judge me for my weakness.

"Dani, help!" I cried to her over the phone in a panic.

"Oh no! What's wrong?"

"I've been pigging out on graham crackers and peanut butter for weeks and it's making me sick, but it's so good and I can't stop!"

This accountability to a friend saved me. I was openly admitting and identifying I had a problem. While I was leap years away from a positive identification of self with food, this act of exposing myself built another tool for my kit—understanding I was powerless over food. I would use it later in life when I got serious about committing forever to the body and health of my dreams.

Minutes after our call, there was a barrage of pounding on my door. Dani had come to the rescue. She stood there in full "perfect girl" regalia: high stack-heeled boots, tight jeans, a fitted sweater, flawless makeup, and her mass of curls magically subdued into obedience.

"Where are they?" she demanded with fire in her eyes as she brushed past me into the kitchen. By the time I caught up with her, there were cabinet doors flying open in every direction.

"Where are they?" she repeated.

"Here," I cringed and pointed to an unsuspecting cabinet.

Dani mercilessly opened the door. "Take them out."

"But . . ."

"Take them out!" Dani showed no mercy.

I reluctantly took out a box of graham crackers and a massive economy-sized jar of smooth Skippy.

"All of it!" She wasn't kidding. I took out the remaining boxes of graham crackers.

"Follow me." She was not playing.

I followed her down the hallway to the incinerator room. She flung open the door, stepped inside, forcefully opened the chute, and looked me dead in the eye.

"Put them in."

"No!" I whimpered.

"Put. Them. In!" Resistance was futile.

I put them in, and Dani shut the chute after the last one. We stood there in silence for another moment before she spotted it. She rolled her eyes, then opened the chute one last time.

"Oh, come on!" I pleaded, as I took my hand out from behind my back. I still had the graham cracker dipped in peanut butter that I was holding when I originally called her.

Dani put her hand on her hip and pursed her lips.

"Ugh, *fine!*" I reluctantly acquiesced.

I put the offending snack into the chute, and Dani closed it and opened it again to make sure it was gone, lest the peanut butter stuck to the metal and I would run back and get it after she left. Yes, I would eat from the trash if desperate enough.

Later in life, I would discover the trick to implementing the accountability strategy is that you have to believe two very important things. One, you must believe that you are worth it. Two, you must believe you are important enough so that the person you are reaching out to will be happy to help and not see you as an annoyance, even if you are seeing them professionally and paying them for their time. Truth be told, there were many times that I did not believe either of those things, and therefore the accountability strategy that I had discovered was left dormant on and off for many years to come.

But one immediate benefit from Dani's intervention was that I never ate graham crackers and peanut butter together ever again after that day. Ever. Oh sure, I see them in the supermarket sometimes, sitting there nonchalantly on the shelf. I act coy, look the other way, and pretend not to see them. Once in a while, I'll even spot them sitting temptingly on a serving platter at a party across a crowded room. I nod and smile politely. But that's it. They were bad for me and I know it. I can even say I once loved them, but it's over. But that doesn't mean I didn't find several new loves in their place.

I was so heavy by the end of graduate school that I took my final exams in sweatpants because they were the only thing that fit me. And at the time, the best remedy I could think of for being tired of being fat was not a healthy daily commitment, but the ultimate sprint: a triathlon. I was in the pool again, but this time add on a racing bike and some serious running sneakers. Are you starting to see a pattern here?

It was also then that I went to my very first private "diet" person to get some help. She was great in that she provided structure around food, and I knew I had to be accountable for what I put in my mouth because I'd have to show up and hop on her scale. But funny enough, I never told her that I privately or publicly binged, which kind of threw a monkey wrench in her helping me because she had no idea what she was dealing with. I never explained the extent of what I was actually going through, and I wouldn't tell anyone until years later when I met Dr. Sacker.

Have you ever been at the point where you just throw your hands up from so many years of trying and think, *Maybe I'm just supposed to be heavy?* If so, you're hardly alone. As I continue to share my journey of ups and downs, we can experience together the work that needs to be done in order to love yourself enough to get to the place that your body and soul have been searching for. When I say "the work," I mean falling flat on my face so many times trying to control my weight, losing control of my weight, and slowly surrendering to the realization that control was never the answer. It was only then that my plan for a happy life with food all came together for me.

I once saw a meme that said, "If you can believe in Santa Clause for eight years, you can probably believe in yourself for five minutes." And that's all it takes: a shift of five minutes to begin to change the course of your life.

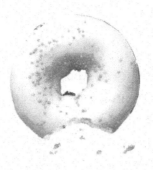

CHAPTER 6

We Gotta Eat!

You know "those people" who just have an aura around them? "Those people" who just walk into a room and you are instantly drawn to them? It could be how they meticulously put themselves together, or maybe they have an enormous energy field that sucks you in and makes you want to linger for a while. Some of them radiate exuberance like sunshine itself, or project majestic confidence, or magically put you at ease and you feel like you can tell them anything. They just have that special something. You're not sure what it is, but you know you want it.

At first, you're excited about making their acquaintance. Surely, you must be destined to connect or you wouldn't feel the pull to do just that. But sometimes the Dark Voice creeps in before you get the chance to connect and convinces you that you're different than they are, and not in a good way. That doubt makes you hesitate, and if you wait long enough, what could have been a beautiful friendship fades into the distance and is replaced by an imaginary massive gulf of worth between the two of you. A perception suggested by the Dark Voice and fabricated in all its glory by your own doubt.

Throughout my lifetime of ups and downs on the scale there were many instances where I kept myself separate from others, believing I wasn't good enough to be their friend or in their circles. This was true for both new and existing friendships alike. Even if I was at my slimmest, the fight with food—and therefore my worth—was alive and well in my head. Sometimes the pull to food was so strong that it knocked the wind out of my lungs and took my feet out from under me. There would literally be *screaming* in my brain that would not stop until the Dark Voice was satisfied half a box of Costco chocolate chip cookies later. I knew "those people" didn't have that pain, and it was in that blatant fact that the gulf of worth between us was validated and cemented in my belief system.

It was always my intention to find my foundation with food so that I could move on in life and finally get off the dress-size roller coaster I was so tightly fastened into. I tried every diet, strategy, method, book, and workout known to man. I even tried going cold turkey, but unlike recreational drugs or cigarettes, food was ever present—not to mention necessary—and used to sanctify the holy days that I held so dear. I mean, we gotta eat, right? There was no way to escape. Food was in my life—in everyone's life—every day, and the vast difference between how food had a hold over me, and how "those people" were their own masters (or so I assumed) crystalized and firmly planted itself in my mind.

In the absence of finding the root cause of my bingeing, no strategy stuck for long. And every new responsibility that was added to my already-overflowing plate seemed to distract me further from the underlying issues I needed to uncover in order to become the person I was meant to be. And that was before my life really took off and I was dealing with more than I ever could have imagined as a newlywed. I was completely unprepared for what would come next.

Alex suggested we buy a house.

I thought he was insane.

"A house? Why on earth do we need a house? It's just the two of us!"

"Because the market is low and it's going to skyrocket in just a few months." He thought the timing was perfect.

But I didn't. A home with no children? A massive purchase that wasn't a necessity? How can you justify something like that? These concepts went against my very strong sense of black and white. Of deserving and not deserving. Of being worthy and not being worthy. The Dark Voice had trained me well.

But after sticking to my guns on this topic for a few days without budging, I suddenly had a different thought. I reminded myself that, at a Jewish wedding, the best blessing you can give the new couple is to build a *bayit ne'eman b'Yisrael*, or "a faithful home among the Jewish people." We give this particular blessing to a young couple establishing a new home because faith is the bedrock, the solid foundation on which everything else is built. It's the one quality mentioned repeatedly throughout the Bible that brings you closer to G-d and eventually saves the day. Even though I really did *not* want to look for a house, I knew that if I didn't step out in faith then I would be sticking my nose up to all of those blessings that everyone had wished us at our wedding seven years ago to build this house in faith. I would be taking Alex's half of those blessings with me. Even though I couldn't do it for myself, I couldn't not do it for him.

So there I was, kicking and screaming, after Alex's insistence just a week later, booked up every Sunday with a real estate agent in the very same neighborhood all of our Jewish couple friends with kids from Forest Hills were now moving. After just a few weeks, we found it. A vintage, cozy, side hall colonial with three bedrooms. It wasn't fancy, but it had good bones and had stood the test of time. The generous covered front porch, nine-foot ceilings, and abundant windows filled each room with light and a relaxed energy. I fell in love. The price was right. My parents were going to help us out. Our offer was accepted. We went into contract. But I was thirty, married for seven years, and had no children yet— not for lack of want or trying—which was beyond alarming in my Orthodox Jewish circles, and was beyond devastating for both Alex and I.

I dragged my feet for almost six months when the line in the sand was drawn. I had to move on even though it was painful, even though I would be different than all of the other women in the suburbs my age with children, even though I felt less than. I knew that in order to create the future of my dreams, I would need to first act in faith and create the space to accommodate a family in complete belief that the children would come. I decided to act "as if." I took a deep breath and whispered goodbye and thank you to our empty apartment that was once filled with all of the joy that comes with the self-assuredness of a perfect future. I gathered my strength, turned around, and listened to the familiar sound of the door shutting behind me and locking into place for the last time.

Living in the suburbs was different. Everyone was over-the-top welcoming. We had so many meals dropped off by friends from Forest Hills that I didn't even know where the supermarket was for the first six weeks we lived there. Even though everyone had extended themselves to make us feel at home and were all about community, I continued to struggle with feeling different, and therefore less worthy. Over the next two years, every yenta in town commented unabashedly on our very personal situation of not yet having children. It was another reminder as to why I didn't want to move in the first place. I loved the idea of moving forward toward positive change, but this was a lot to take. I had always used my body to make it do what I wanted it to do. Binge. Sprint. Get a master's degree. Run a triathlon. And now I found myself in a place where I needed to surrender to not having control because I couldn't make my body do what I wanted it to do and have a baby. Surrendering control was not in my vernacular at that time, even though you'd think it would have been because of my deep connection with G-d. But the Dark Voice was speaking so loudly and clogging my brain with so many thoughts of failure and not-good-enough and *you're different* that my faith was compromised.

The suburbs were an entirely different galaxy. You drove to the supermarket instead of walking with your granny wagon. Women *dressed* for the day in designer clothing with a full face of makeup and perfectly coiffed hair instead of hanging out in jeans, sneakers, and a ponytail. Things were a lot fancier in this place my friend refers to as the "gilded ghetto." Women my age didn't work and stayed home with children and had housekeepers. But they didn't "stay home." I couldn't find anyone to go rollerblading with me through the streets to explore my new neighborhood because everyone was busy meeting for coffee, shopping on the avenue while pushing their super-expensive strollers with their designer purses, or getting their six-month-old babies together for play dates. Most of the women who did work had flex hours and worked for themselves, where they could just create their own schedules instead of having a traditional nine-to-five, which was a glamorous concept I had never really heard of. And they had perfect figures.

The overwhelming majority of women looked awesome even though they'd given birth multiple times, were constantly lunching with the ladies and entertaining every Sabbath, their homes filled with decadent foods. I felt like I had just landed on Mars and I needed to be taken to the Mothership to learn the strange and mysterious ways of these fabulous-looking aliens. And everyone had kids. *Everyone.*

As is the long-standing tradition in Jewish neighborhoods, we were immediately invited over by several different families almost every Sabbath after services to enjoy a meal. We were never the only couple there. The large majority of homes we were invited to were overwhelmingly grand, exquisitely decorated, and could easily accommodate entertaining a few families at once quite comfortably.

One particular Sabbath, we were invited to the home of a friend from Forest Hills for lunch along with three other couples with their children. There were endless courses of perfectly prepared dishes. These women must have worked tirelessly at creating incredibly elegant tables where everyone felt welcomed, and to their credit they pulled it off with ease. I truly didn't know how they did it because every time I did it, which was often, it never worked out for me like it did for these ladies. Oh sure, I'd make all the food and my table would look incredible and everyone would ooh and aah about how fabulous the food was. But what Sabbath is really about is *Shabbat Menucha*, which means that we are supposed to "rest" on Sabbath or have a "cessation from work." However, in my traditional Jewish household in modern times, this day seemed busier than ever because I had exhausted myself by staying up until all hours Thursday night to prepare a million and one complicated and impressive dishes for my company so that I could work a full day on Friday. This caused me high levels of undue stress, staying home from synagogue Sabbath morning to set the table, cut up the various salads, heat up the food, and run around the house like a banshee tidying up last minute before everyone arrived. Then when everyone came I'd be sweating, annoyed, and up and down on my feet, serving and cleaning up course after course after course. Everyone would linger for hours, and the food wars started in my head, and I inevitably ended up in a public bingeing marathon because I was tired and stressed and didn't know if I was coming or going and could in no way keep my head about me.

But these women had a completely different air about them. They were so put together, relaxed, and lovely, and we were welcomed with warm open arms. They were more interested in getting to know us than shoving the food on the table in their mouths, and possessed magical powers to sit back and do just that. I was eager to do my part, and when the main course was over, my hostess finally agreed to my endless offers to help her clear the table. I was rolling up my sleeves in anticipation of washing up the dishes, but upon entering the kitchen I found someone was already standing at the sink, having beaten me to it. Funny, I hadn't seen her at the table. And don't judge, but it took me a minute to realize that it was her housekeeper. *Ohh, so that's her secret.* I didn't grow up with help of any kind in the house. This was my very first encounter with this type of arrangement, and it hit me in the face like a ton of bricks. These people actually felt worthy enough to ask for help in their lives. Not because it was a necessity, but because it would make their lives better and aid in keeping down their stress levels so they could give themselves the gift of self-care and have an enjoyable outcome. They actually felt they deserved it, and that it wasn't a sin not to run yourself into the ground. Shocking, but eye opening at the same time. Actual *Shabbat Menucha*. I didn't know if I was horrified at the audacity of it all, or if I had just found the answer to life's greatest mystery. What a concept: asking for help that wasn't for an overt necessity but just to make things more pleasant for yourself and to bring you to that relaxed state that you're after. Interesting. I'd have to make a mental note of that.

I helped my hostess bring in the rest of the dishes, and we

brought the endless array of desserts to the table to accommodate her twenty guests before sitting down. The food was decadent, the company was wonderful, and the conversation continued to flow easily until it was interrupted by an older guest.

"So *nu*? Why don't you have children already?" she questioned me loudly from across the table.

The table fell silent. Nobody moved. My mouth fell open, but no sound came out. The stark contrast between how I lived my life and the other women who were supposedly my contemporaries in my Jewish neighborhood was growing by leaps and bounds. My heart hurt. All I could hear was a voice in my head saying, *Welcome to the suburbs. Pass the cake, please.*

Alex saved us all.

"Well, you see, it's my fault," he began sheepishly. "I lost my testicles in the war."

Dead silence followed by uncontrollable laughter. My hero.

There would be a lot of moments like that over the next two years.

I got calls from complete strangers saying that they heard about me from so-and-so, and they knew of an excellent doctor or an infertility support group and had a friend I could go with.

Or this: "Hi, Naomi! Did you hear, Rebecca's pregnant with her third! Oh . . . I'm so sorry! Should I have said that to you?"

We were asked thirty-five times to attend circumcisions and carry the newborn baby to the pulpit in synagogue, as it is said to give merit to have a child of our own. After seeing Alex walk down the aisle with a new baby three times in one week, the confused father of a friend approached him and asked, "What are you? A sperm donor?"

One Sabbath after services, I was standing in the lobby of my enormous synagogue when a friend that went to my high school rushed over. I was so happy to see that she was excited to say hello because our friendship had changed. She had just had her first child. I felt that people were on a different life path than me, that I was getting pushed out of friendships and being replaced by play dates. Seeing her broad smile and long, dark hair swaying as she hurried toward me made me realize that it was just my imagination. As I basked in the warmth of her smile, I wondered if my original perception of my feelings of inadequacy and not belonging in this fresh and novel environment was all wrong. Clearly, this smile meant I belonged. How could it mean otherwise? And if I belonged, it meant I would figure out the food too. I bet everyone started in this neighborhood just like me, with similar struggles, and needed to figure how to navigate the overwhelming amount of food while looking like supermodels. Surely, that smile meant we were all in this together and that she, along with everyone else in this lobby, was sending skinny karma and baby thoughts my way. They were all empowering me, and I was just being paranoid and silly.

I pulled her into a close hug, and she hugged me back. But then she didn't let go. She slipped something in my hand and whispered in my ear, "I was cleaning out the cabinet under the sink in my bathroom and found this unopened fertility kit with a bunch of pregnancy test sticks and an ovulation chart. Clearly, I don't need it anymore, but I figured you could use it."

And with that, she turned and left me standing in the midst of hundreds of families holding a transparent plastic CVS bag with a fertility kit for everyone to see.

Nope, my theory was not just my imagination.

Alex finally found me just a few seconds later.

"Hey, what's in the bag?"

"Someone just gave me a fertility kit."

We stood there looking at each other, nodding our heads, trying to wrap our brains around the entirety of our situation.

"You think they have anything good in the *kiddush*?" I asked. "All of a sudden I feel like having cookies."

It came to the point where not a day went by that there was not a comment or a well-intentioned person to remind me that I was different, that what I wanted to achieve was beyond me, and that there wasn't anything I could do about it.

As I wasn't busy with children at home, I immersed myself in my work at school and took on several private cases in the early evenings, many of whom lived in my neighborhood. So there I was, childless, wishing for children, and spending my evenings taking care of the children of the very well-intentioned people actively reminding me of my own current bleak reality. And just to remind you once again, my specialty was feeding therapy for children. Meanwhile, the child in me had still not come to terms with her core wounds, and was abusing food. Oh, the irony.

I worked in several different schools over a twenty-plus-year span with some of our community's most compromised students. And the truth of the matter is that these children saved me every day. I could jump into helping those amazing kids and not think about the Dark Voice in my head. I would be binge-and-sprint-free in those hours. I could go into work and be in the worst funk ever and just want to sit and cry, but I couldn't help but smile when I picked up my first kid for therapy.

These kids have such big hearts and just want love. And they are hysterical in their innocence and unabashed in how they are completely unencumbered from the doubts the rest of us allow to limit our special light. They make me laugh so hard! Sometimes as they have me in stitches, I'll turn to one of the other therapists and say, "I can't even believe they pay me to do this." My job is the best gig ever. It's about putting all your heart and soul into someone so deserving without receiving anything in return. The other therapists make fun of me that my favorites are the louder kids.

I guess I feel akin to them. Some days, I will get punched or hit or bitten or kicked. I've gotten scratched, spit at, thrown up and peed on, but I keep coming back for more. And I fight for them. I fight for their progress and their future so that they may have the best quality of life possible and be a contributing member of society. I fight so they can be self-sufficient and enjoy all the pleasures of life.

We gotta eat, right? But exactly how do we want to feed ourselves? How come I could spend every waking professional day facilitating healthy eating for all of these kids, but I couldn't seem to do the same for myself?

The answer came like a lightning bolt to the head one day as I was teaching a student at a school on Staten Island how to drink from a cup. His mom had sent in a chocolate-flavored meal supplement that day. Now I wanted a chocolate shake. I mean, I did deserve it, right? I'd pick up something similar for myself on the way home. So there I was, helping this adorable kid and deciding if I wanted chocolate sauce or peanut butter when I looked into his big, brown, puppy-dog eyes. He consecutively swallowed two full sips and gave me the biggest smile filled with pride at his accomplishment. All at once I felt ashamed, like a complete self-absorbed idiot, and beyond grateful for this long-overdue revelation. If he could find joy and pride in his relationship with food, then there was hope for me. Just being in that child's presence had taught me so much more than I could ever teach him. Not that all of a sudden I felt fabulous about myself, or my relationship with food, or my childless situation, but he certainly had put things in perspective and gave me two more skills to put in my toolbox: gratitude for the challenges I'd been given, and unwavering faith in what will surely be the bright future that awaits.

As time passed, my faith, belief, and trust that the family I dreamed of would be delivered took over how I originally felt. I knew in the depths of my soul that our "faithful home among the Jewish people" would soon be built. I just knew it. It was like I was back at the swim meet at NYU when I started laughing during that unforgettable last lap. Grit came to me again. Summer reappeared. Comparison to "those people" took a new form, and I slowly started to see what I was going through from a place of self-love, acceptance, and now gratitude. Gratitude for the excruciating challenges I was sent to bear because they held the greatest rewards. And with grit and unwavering faith that G-d ran the world for the good of everyone, I began to persist courageously in the face of my darkest fears and the instances of my deepest doubts, even if it wasn't a consistent part of my repertoire just yet. My courage and faith pushed me to take action in a way I will never regret one Passover at my parents' home on Staten Island.

We had taken a break from pursuing the fertility path for the past six months, as it had become all-consuming and completely overwhelming. What was supposed to be spontaneous and exciting was becoming a real drag. We needed some mental space.

The seder was over, and I reflected on its theme of freedom and what freedom means to me. Free to pursue our destinies. Free to believe in our futures. To shed whatever oppresses you, and to know with unwavering faith that G-d will split the rough waters so that you can walk through on your own and you will come out on the other side unharmed and victorious.

I finished helping my mom clear the table and put the dishes away, then went to my childhood bedroom where Alex was starting to fall asleep. The same bedroom where I cried myself to sleep over my own personal oppressions, and where I prayed for my own personal freedoms and redemptions so many times before.

"Did you enjoy the seder?" I asked.

"Yeah, it was great. Sorry I didn't help you clean up. I'm exhausted from all that wine."

We both giggled.

"Alex?"

"Yeah."

"Alex, we've tried everything. We've tried every method, every pill, and every surgery. The only thing left is IVF. I know it's a lot, but I'm ready to go for it if you are. I'm thirty-one, and my odds of getting pregnant are starting to diminish with each passing year, and it will get increasingly difficult if we want to have more children down the road. There's no guarantee when and if it's going to work, but . . . let's find out. If you're not into it right now, I totally get it and we'll just drop the whole thing, or maybe get on adoption lists if that sounds good to you. But I'm ready. I'm ready to go for the future. What do you say?"

"I'm in. Let's do it."

I held my breath and tried not to cry.

"Happy Passover, baby."

"Happy Passover."

And we dove head first into the unknown.

CHAPTER 7

Who Do You Think You Are, Anyway?

A lbert Einstein is credited as saying, "The definition of insanity is doing the same thing over and over again and expecting different results." Although I would repeat my cycle of binge eating for over forty years, my desire for change led me to learn many lessons with regard to self-correction, failure, and success. Each one filled me with a little more hope. What about you? Have you ever learned from a past experience and created a completely different outcome the second time around? What have you turned around for the better that was once so ingrained in your psyche?

For example, let's say you come home stressed from work and let off steam by yelling at your significant other. Later that night, you feel remorseful, apologize, and promise it will never happen again. The next time you come home stressed from work, you remember how terrible you felt after yelling at your significant other, and decide to go for a walk instead. Same event, different outcome.

With binge and sprint, I had to repeat sticking my finger in the proverbial electric socket until the umpteenth time when I finally figured it out. No matter where you currently are with eating or any other challenge in your life, keep going until you change your habits instead of allowing a set of repeated behaviors to mindlessly lead you. Get strong where you can and build from there. Proverbs 24:16 says, "For though the righteous fall seven times, they rise again." And although the Dark Voice may try its damnedest to make you feel unworthy and ask, "Who do you think you are, anyway?" remember that you are surely among the righteous, and that you have complete capacity to rise again. I was successful in co-creating such a scenario with G-d's help after one of the most challenging ordeals of my life.

IVF wasn't working. I was on my third cycle and I felt nothing. Nothing! *This can't be happening,* I thought. We were a nice Jewish couple who just wanted babies. Being barren wasn't in my playbook. The week before, I was sitting in synagogue listening to a guest speaker present in place of the rabbi's usual sermon, waiting for him to say something I could hold onto, a little spark of hope that would carry me through the week. It was as if I willed his speech into existence because he then spoke about having children, but then the message went awry.

"A person without children is only half a person," he said.

I froze in my seat, and I felt the tensing bodies of people sitting near me, their eyes glued to the guest speaker, afraid to accidentally glance in my direction. I thought I was going to throw up right there in the aisle, and it took every ounce of strength in my body not to start crying for everyone to see. The guest speaker, of course, had no intention of making me personally feel bad, as he didn't even know me, but I was so vulnerable to believing I was broken. His sentiment was an exact reflection of what I knew to be true for me. I was only living half a life without a child. Now, of course, I know many women can't have children, or haven't had children due to their life circumstances, or have made the decision not to have children, and they are completely secure and whole in who they are in this world. They nurture many other people and accomplishments. But I personally wanted my identification to be complete with children, and my whole heart ached at the thought of not achieving that state. There I was after my third IVF cycle—the final cycle that insurance would pay for—and I felt nothing. I was devastated and scared, and I couldn't even begin to fathom how we would pay the exorbitant fees on our own for another cycle.

That night after dinner, I said *Birkat Hamazon*, or "Grace After Meals," which is said after eating bread, and I finally uncovered what my doubt was intended to make me realize. At the end of Grace After Meals, this quote from Genesis 24:1 appears in the prayer book: "Now Abraham was old, well on in his years, and G-d blessed Abraham with everything." Rashi, a French medieval rabbi who composed a comprehensive commentary on the Bible and beyond, pointed out that the numerical value of the Hebrew word for *with everything* has the same numerical value as the word *son*, indicating that all of Abraham's good fortune was worthless to him until G-d finally blessed him with a child in his old age. I stared at it as if it were the first time I was ever seeing it, and I instinctively flipped back to the middle of Grace After Meals and found this corresponding line: "Just as Abraham, Isaac, and Jacob were blessed in everything, from everything, and with everything, so may He bless us all together with a perfect blessing." The commentaries note that the word *everything* implies perfection, a total unflawed blessing. The enormity of what I had just realized left me breathless. Even though I'd been saying this prayer after eating bread for my entire life, I had never made the connection that this was, in fact, a blessing whose roots are in having a child, embedded within the context of food. So there I was, praying for a child with every bite of bread for the entirety of my life, and at the same time fighting the bread (especially challah bread), which represents sustenance and is an integral part of the cultivation of the child. The blessings were clearly connected. My faith was telling me that nourishment and childbearing go hand in hand, but I'd been fighting half the prayer for as long as I could remember, and in turn keeping what I'd been praying for away from me all this time.

In an attempt to right the error of my ways, I said that passage once more, but this time my *kavanah* was fully focused on the entire prayer, and I asked G-d to bestow His limitless bounty upon Alex and me with a child that we may nourish in the most beautiful way possible.

The next morning, my long-awaited news was finally delivered. Positive! The pregnancy test was *positive!* Oh happy day! There were babies floating on clouds, and storks flying my way, and fireworks exploding wherever I looked, and I got down on my knees and I screamed *thank you* at the top of my lungs repeatedly until I had no voice left, through tears of joy and pain and gratitude and release that I thought would never stop. Our baby was coming! That must have been a really powerful prayer because we found out six weeks later that it was two babies. We were having twins! I swore right then and there in a moment of overwhelming gratitude that I was going to be perfect with my food during my pregnancy so that my babies were nourished with the precise nutrients they needed. My food intake would be as perfect as the blessing that was bestowed upon us. Had I ever been pregnant with twins before, I would have known that it would be a broken vow that I would have to atone for the next Yom Kippur.

I waited until my fifth month before I would agree to tell

anyone we were expecting. Alex was so excited to tell everyone the good news, urging me to trust the Universe and share our joy.

"Naomi, we're well past the first trimester. When do you want to start telling people already?"

"Um . . . when they're in college?" was my honest reply. Alex knew me better than I knew myself. He clearly saw my fears. And as usual, he supported me in every way by creating a world of safety around me just by being his strong, reliable, consistent, loving self. Without having to say a word, he waited patiently for me to come around. He was my rock, my hero.

I was petrified this long-awaited double gift would be taken from us, but I couldn't stay in that negative mind space because, by default, that would mean that Alex would have to stay in that mind space. He was ready to share his joy with the world. Who was I to stop him from having that experience? It wasn't fair for me to delay him any longer because my fear was too great. Not this time. The stakes were way too high. I needed to step out in faith. No matter how fast I would run, I was powerless over the ultimate fate of our babies. I needed to take G-d's hand and pray that would be enough. The old cycle of being afraid that something bad was going to happen to offset the abundance in my life—like a ledger of Naomi destiny—was in full force with having children. I decided to follow Alex's lead of unshakeable faith and take the plunge. And guess what? Telling people made me feel more confident that a favorable outcome would come my way. And the more people we told, the happier I got, and that joy magically dispelled all the fear of something being taken away. It was almost as if the compounding joy of each new recipient of this incredible news validated our deserving of it, and the looming threats of the Dark Voice had no choice but to recoil in turn. We didn't need to keep our babies a secret like I did all the thoughts about my weight, or cower in the dark kitchen while soothing myself with food. With each call, I became more confident and assured that everything would be just fine.

I had waited and prayed and worked so hard for this, and I felt this was our destiny and we deserved it. I had paid my dues and now it was our turn. I became emboldened and started knocking on doors and telling my good friends in person. People hugged me and cried and told me that we had been on countless prayer lists, even more prayers than we had known about. We had never received such an outpouring of love. Who would have thought that all of these people were supporting us in humility, quietly doing something beautiful for us and not even telling us. It was another gold star of absolute grace on the checklist of the women in my neighborhood who knew how to live in their beauty. They weren't ashamed to ask for help to continue living in a way they were accustomed to and believed they rightfully deserved. Apparently, they were also pretty good at looking beyond themselves and taking the initiative to help others—the type of help that went way beyond inviting someone for lunch, or the help that they would never even get credit or acknowledgement for from the person they were helping. And in turn, it seemed that feeling worthy was my ticket to joy as well. In that moment, I felt free to immerse myself with abandon in all that life had given us, and it was absolutely glorious. It was a high that I had never experienced before. Feeling worthy of joy is the goal because when you are in that moment, you are unstoppable. I felt so grateful for Alex's complete understanding and foresight of exactly what I needed.

My newfound excitement gave me the gumption to call and tell my eight-year-old niece that she would soon have a new cousin.

"Hi, sweetie! I have such good news! We're going to have a baby, and you're going to have a new cousin!"

"Oh yay! I'm so excited. But Aunt Naomi, you were so skinny, and now you're going to be fat."

What? I felt something back in the recesses of my mind rear its ugly head.

"No . . . I mean, the baby grows in the mommy's tummy, but then the baby comes out and you get skinny again," I explained.

"No, you won't. All mommies who have babies are fat."

I kind of laughed, trying not to project on an eight-year-old. "No they're not, silly. There are lots of mommies who are thin."

"No there aren't." She was completely convinced that she was right. And as much as I endeavored to keep down the fears she was bringing up and not argue with a child, I couldn't help myself.

"Well, I have a friend who has four babies, and she's very thin."

My niece was silent for a moment. "Well," she retorted, "then she's not Jewish!"

I laughed, but in the back of my mind, I was afraid of her prediction. Look, from what I hear, most people who are pregnant with twins just want to eat. They succumb to the inevitable, and then like a "normal" person, they go back to their normal eating and regain their normal figures. But I wasn't a normal person with food that had normal concerns about weight. So, what my niece said freaked me out considerably, and I became extra meticulous about my diet, reinforcing my determination to gain only what was necessary. I had sought out "private diet lady" help before, but being pregnant was different. I was forced to find an actual nutritionist because, as it turned out, I was one of those fainting pregnant ladies and needed to be watched to up my protein and other nutrients I needed to keep me vertical during the day. But once she set a diet for me that worked, I felt I no longer needed her, and I was set free to face the rest of my pregnancy on my own.

Even though I had made a mental note of being like all those women from the neighborhood that I so admired who asked for help, at the time I believed that I was supposed to muscle through all the pain and conflict that overeating caused within me and not talk to anyone about it. Why did I do this? Maybe I didn't think I was worthy of a game plan or conversation. Perhaps I hadn't admitted to myself that I actually had a real issue with stress and food. I also didn't feel I deserved to spend money on myself, especially with two babies on the way, but then I would binge because I wasn't spending money on myself and needed to subconsciously fill that void. Plus, if I was on a binge, then getting help was a non-issue because there was no stopping that train once it was in motion. It was a vicious cycle. I wouldn't give myself what I needed to be at peace, so the Dark Voice grew stronger with the proof that I wasn't worth the money, which caused me to eat more than I should, which was more proof, and round and round I went.

So, what do you think happened after a few months? You know it, the twin eating fest commenced, and I turned the tables from careful-eating pregnant lady to shoving-the-whole-world-in-my-face pregnant lady, and I was starting to get comments about how many babies I actually had in there. Turns out, one doesn't overcome a lifetime of conditioning after one episode of feeling worthy and joyousness no matter how impactful it is. The real test is when life offers conflict and unexpected turmoil, and in this case, new experiences.

At the end of the summer when I was off from school for a few weeks prior to the fall semester, I would eat a huge lunch at home, and then go to the avenue to do errands. Once I was there, I would see friends.

"Hi! Oh wow, you look great!"

"Thanks, I'm getting really excited."

"Hey, we were just going to lunch, have you eaten yet?"

"No! I'd love to join you!"

Lunch number two, and I ordered dessert too.

The scale started rapidly tipping, but I was powerless to stop it. It's hard to tell how you actually look when you're pregnant, especially in the warmer weather. All you have to do is put on flip-flops and a mumu, and you're good to go. It's not like you're getting into jeans or a heavy coat or stockings, so how can you really tell? I mean, you're supposed to be growing. You're pregnant, for goodness' sake! And it wasn't like I had a point of reference. I had never been pregnant before, much less pregnant with twins.

The night before the magical day arrived, Alex insisted we make a video, telling our babies how long awaited they were, and how we could already feel the joy of meeting them.

"Alex, now? I have a million things to do to get ready!"

"Yes, now," he chuckled, and gently led me to the video camera he had set up. "If not now, when? Just sit down and relax. You'll be so happy you did."

And, of course, he was right. That's Alex, always balancing my sprint by slowing me down, making sure I take in the joys of life, unassumingly wrestling me away from my endless list of things to be accomplished with his practical jokes, and distracting me with his unexpected humor and wit, reducing me to a puddle of tears from laughing so hard. To this day, that video is one of my most treasured memories.

I awoke the next morning with a jolt. We were going to meet our babies! We couldn't wait to find out if they were boys or girls. What color hair would they have? Whom would they look like? How much would they weigh? What would it feel like to hold them? My heart was pounding out of my chest with anticipation, but we needed to make a quick stop at the bay before we went to the hospital.

Because I was on house arrest (a.k.a. bed rest) for the last month of my high-risk pregnancy, I waited until the last day of the Jewish holiday Sukkot, and therefore the last possible day to say the prayer *tashlich*, which literally translates to "cast away." Chabad defines *tashlich* as "symbolically casting our sins into the water and leaving our old shortcomings behind us, thus starting the Jewish new year with a clean slate." I could not think of a more appropriate way to start our lives with our new babies. Alex helped me out of the car, and I could feel his strength as he patiently waited for me at the edge of the water to complete my prayers.

From the straits did I call upon G-d, G-d answered me with expansiveness.

G-d is with me, I have no fear . . .

The prayer couldn't be any more perfect. And as I cast my bread into the water, I threw with it all of the bingeing, the overwhelming fear of loss, the need to control, and the not-good-enough with all my might. Even though all of those things would still follow me for years to come, I was slowly becoming more and more aware, chipping away at it ever so slowly and steadily.

I strutted into the hospital perfectly coiffed and picture-ready for our twins' debut. All of my friends talked about their horror stories of panting, sweating, and pushing for hours on end, but I was scheduled for a C-section, made necessary by my prior lady surgeries. We walked up to the front desk and said, "Hi. The Josephs for Dr. Silver. We're his eleven o'clock birth. We'll have a seat over there." Ah, so civilized.

And then the moment I was avoiding directly after emerging from the changing room donning a cap and hospital gown. The scale.

"Oh, I know around how much I weigh."

"We need an exact weight for your epidural."

Hmmm. Can't fudge that one.

Reluctantly, I stepped up on the scale. This was one of those major milestone moments in my life, and I could not bear to be reminded of the destruction I had caused myself from all of the non-stop eating I had done over the past several months. Not that I could see my feet or the dial on the scale from my vantage point. By this time, I was as wide as I was tall. But it seemed that all the stars were aligned and to my relief, there was no monitor showing the patient how much their weight was. Well, as long as the doctor knows. This was supposed to be the happiest day of my life. Why bother me with the details? While standing on the scale, I heard the faint pieces of information coming from behind the glass wall about different patients.

"Ready for epidural in room four."

"Nurse needed in OR B."

"Section in recovery room two."

And then they announced a number reflecting a patient's weight.

I stood on the scale and wondered whom they were speaking about. I thought about all of the women who just brought life into the world and wondered if any of them were like me. Were they having twins? Did they try for all those years? Did they have the yearning in their hearts like I did? What about the woman whose weight they announced? Her weight wasn't a lot by any stretch of the imagination for a taller woman, but for me standing under five-three with a smaller-than-average bone structure? Just the number itself made me giggle. I couldn't imagine what I would look like at that weight, nine months pregnant with twins or not! Ridiculous.

A nurse helped me down from the scale and onto a gurney to wheel me into delivery. Alex was waiting just outside the doors, and he held my hand as we wheeled silently down the hall. As usual, we didn't need to exchange words. We could feel the pain and the joy of the past ten years silently being transmitted through our hearts. It was the most peaceful moment of my life. A lifelong dream about to be fulfilled . . . and then I saw it. In bright red numbers on the chart at the foot of my bed.

That number they announced was *my* weight.

Really? Now? Of all times to affront me with my greatest, darkest challenge. Come on, Universe! I was beyond pissed off that my lifelong battle and immortal foe had strong-armed their way into the most beautiful, meaningful moment of my life, completely unwanted and uninvited. How dare they! How dare this number sidetrack me and take me away from the beauty of this moment. *Can't I have one single minute where this bingeing can't follow me? Where I can just rest for one second?*

"You okay there? You look far away," Alex interrupted the barrage of thoughts rushing their way through my nervous system. *How does he always know? Man, he's good.*

"I was, but I'm back."

He gave me a wink, I squeezed his hand, and just like that I let G-d in and all the distracting thoughts melted away. We were going to meet our babies! The doors opened, and we were whisked into the delivery room.

We had a boy and a girl, in that order. Sammy and Serena. They were absolute perfection, and we were drunk with pure joy. And as they wheeled me into recovery, and I clicked the morphine clicker with abandon to make sure I was pain-free enough to care for my new twins, I couldn't help but imagine what would have happened if I hadn't discussed IVF with Alex that Passover night and found out that we both wanted it so desperately. Wayne Gretzky is attributed to saying, "You miss one hundred percent of the shots you don't take." What if I had not taken my grit and stamina and applied them to almost a decade of trying everything possible to fill the dream of having a family? Regardless of whether or not the desire to have babies came from filling a hole, I knew in that moment the desire was pure.

What about you, dear reader? What do you want so badly but stopped asking for it because the road to your fantasy has become so overwhelmingly arduous? I urge you, take it back out, dust it off, look at it, and realize it's worth fighting for because you are worth having it. A creative dream, an adventure, that guy or girl at work you want to ask out, a raise, or even children. You may think it's impossible, but I believe that if you want it—if you have that desire in you—then it was put there to force you out of your comfort zone and push you to grow and not stop until you get it. You can do it imperfectly. You can do it with food issues, weight struggles, and low self-worth. Because when you get what you need, the issues with food will start to heal as you heal yourself. Why else would that desire be in your soul? It's your sign that it's for you, and that it's in your power to get it. So stay in the game and keep going. Don't bench yourself. And while I'm so glad I can give that advice to you in hindsight, I was in no way able to put it into practice at the time.

When we arrived home, our friends and cousins were waiting for us on the lawn. They had completely transformed our home, and it was in full party regalia for the *Shalom Zachor*, which means to welcome the male baby. Long tables were set up and filled with decadent dishes and desserts and bottles of wine dropped off by neighbors who would gather later that night in celebration. I was struck by the caring of the women in the neighborhood who so carefully cared for themselves, and in turn had the wherewithal to care for others.

I went upstairs and showered for the first time in days, and got into a not-too-obvious maternity dress. I made my way downstairs to hear the rabbi speak and was greeted by dozens of friends and well-wishers who had walked in the dark to offer their congratulations and make our celebration all that it could be. I had dreamed of this moment for so many years, and I was so beyond appreciative of everyone who was there but I couldn't take it all in. I couldn't adequately express my gratitude, and I certainly couldn't enjoy it. All I could think was that I needed to get my incision to bed and that the babies were waiting to be fed. I was already sprinting away from becoming the elegant example every woman in my home had set for me, and settling in for a long haul of being under the thumb of the Dark Voice of not deserving. And the binge was there as well as I quickly perused the table of desserts from a bird's-eye view as I climbed the stairs, preparing in my mind what I would have when they were all gone.

And thus began life with the twins.

There is a Jewish tradition that you're not supposed to have the baby's room set up until it is born. A "don't count your chickens before they're hatched" type of thing. Apparently, I was the only one in the neighborhood who didn't get the memo about two popular hacks to this rule: One, go to the baby store, put everything on hold, and then have it all delivered to your house prior to returning from the hospital. Two, set everything up except for a few items so that the baby's room is not technically complete. Even if I was aware of these hacks, I probably wouldn't have taken action because I was on bedrest the entire month before the twins' due date (and this was before online shopping!), I hadn't even heard of the concept of "registering," and nothing could have prepared me for how overwhelming it was to have twins. So, maybe you'll understand why I started our new life as a family with two babies, no nursery, no changing table, and no furniture. And I take full responsibility. Alex had less of a clue than I did, and as a guy who lived in an apartment with a bunch of fraternity brothers in college, he wasn't really bothered by the mess. He was just following my lead as I continuously assured him that "I got it!" even though I clearly didn't, and in no way could I admit it to myself, much less to Alex.

I only had the formula and bottles from the hospital, but I believed that I would be an expert at nursing and wouldn't need them. I mean, I *am* a specialist in pediatric feeding and swallowing, for goodness' sake! The result of this non-planning? Baby paraphernalia flying everywhere. Our bedroom was like a dorm room in a frat house except the clothes were much smaller, and there were stinky diapers in the place of empty beer cans. This was one of the major reasons for my post-partum depression. I felt like I was buried under an avalanche of baby slop that was continuously raining down on my head, and I couldn't get out from under it. I thought of the pristine, relaxed, put-together nurseries of my neighborhood friends, and the disparity between us became an overwhelming abyss.

And the nursing . . . let's revisit that for a moment. There was a lesson that I learned from nursing that can be applied in many different ways, and it doesn't need to be nursing for you to apply this lesson to your life. Think about any project that you undertook that completely threw you into Tuesday of next month. Where you had to work through something that you perceived as non-negotiable and tortured your very soul every step of the way.

Turns out that, unbeknownst to me, I was allergic to all that morphine I was clicking into my bloodstream after the delivery. My body had an awful reaction, and by the time I had slept it off, the twins had been bottle-fed several times and no longer wanted to nurse. Add in the fact that my body was not producing the amount of milk required for one baby, much less two, and it was a recipe for disaster. Now, had I been in my right mind I would have continued bottle-feeding, nursed whatever I could, focused on the joy of having twins, and moved on. But as soon as we returned home, I hit the ground running in the hardest sprint of my life with thousands of dollars and months spent on lactation consultants, schedules, charts, different methods, different techniques, and different equipment that culminated in the ultimate feelings of stress, failure, and not living up to expectations. Once again, I could not make my body do what I wanted it to do. It was a trifecta grand slam for the Dark Voice, as it taunted me relentlessly for not measuring up in the areas of feeding, eating, and nourishment, the simplest, most natural G-d-given things a mother is supposed to organically provide for her children and herself.

I was so affected by this turmoil that each time I would try to nurse or pump, there was this "synapse" that connected in my brain, and instantaneously every single upsetting or unsettling thought or feeling rushed together in an avalanche to the front of my forehead and bile would rise up in the back of my throat. I could hear the Dark Voice loud and clear: "Who do you think you are, anyway? You have your children, and now you can't even feed them! Clearly, you're not worthy of the gifts you've been given! Clearly, you don't deserve to take care of yourself!"

I was finally a mother like everyone else, yet I couldn't sprint away from the feelings of alienation and loneliness I thought having children would rid me of. My only temporary escape from these feelings were provided by visitors. When well-wishers dropped by with gifts, I could catch a glimpse of what it was that they saw. The beauty and blessings that had been bestowed upon me so graciously and abundantly. During those times, it was as if I emerged from a dark cave and could gasp for air, filling my lungs with momentary joy and sunshine and sustenance and beauty. But the moment they left, down I would fall, back to being completely engulfed by the suffocating darkness.

I lost about fourteen pounds from giving birth (I have no

idea how that worked out mathematically as each baby was over six pounds, but whatever). I was at the highest weight I had ever been without being pregnant and I didn't even look like myself. I was completely unrecognizable. I started identifying as Bessie the Cow. I was constantly nursing around the clock, so I was starving and didn't bother to feed myself in the healthiest of ways, connecting the binge to the sprint. Clearly, I didn't think I was worthy of spending the time or money on myself to seek out assistance from a nutritionist. I began to sink deeper and deeper into post-partum depression, and it didn't help that I felt like every single alien hormone that I had pumped into my body during IVF was once again being released into my system after giving birth.

After five months, on March 4, I went back to work. (How ironic is that? March Forth!) The guilt that I felt leaving the twins was only matched by the guilt of feeling overwhelmed when I walked in the door after my work day was done. Some days I was so tired I just wanted to lie down when I came home, but I felt too guilty doing that. What mother doesn't immediately scoop up her kids and instantly come alive at the sight of them after being away from them for an entire day? Some days I would sit in my driveway for fifteen minutes getting up the courage to walk into the house. There was one time that I was beyond exhausted. I needed to lie down, but I knew I couldn't do that once I went home. So I went to the only other place I felt at peace. Loehmann's. I parked my minivan in the Loehmann's parking lot, lay down in the back, and took a forty-minute nap. It was the most glorious thing I was able to remember doing for myself in a long time.

It didn't help matters any that I was still eating enough to feed a large cow and that nothing fit me. I was literally dressing in whatever stretchy "rags" I had in my closet or, as we say in Yiddish, *shmatas*. I looked and felt awful, and I refused to buy any clothes that would fit someone of my size. Forget that I was a human female who just had two live people come out of her body who deserved to be clothed properly until it was time for her body to return to normal. No way was I going to give in to that kind of weak thinking! I was hard on myself. I had no compassion. I never thought for a moment that I should find other women experiencing the same pain. I didn't read books about feeling better, and I couldn't even fathom allowing myself to nurture and care for the heavier woman I was who had gone through quite an ordeal with three IVFs and twins and now back to work.

Looking back, I wish I had taken the example of the gracious women in my neighborhood who ditched the *shmatas*, adapted lacy Wonderbras into nursing bras, used Chanel wraps to drape around their babies as a cover-up while nursing, not to mention dressing themselves in designer clothing, perfectly procured accessories, and finding a dietician. But I didn't see myself as worthy of those things. I was dressed in *shmatas* and hadn't showered in a week. Where was the mothership? Did I miss the memo on how to thrive in many areas at once? Because I was totally missing the mark.

But let me just spell it out straight: In no way did the women in my neighborhood make me feel bad about my state of being at all. They only stood as shining examples of what I wanted to achieve, but I completely just couldn't get it, and it was within that construct of comparison that I felt the widening gap of separation between myself and these role models. As it turns out, sometimes what we need the most help with is where we are the weakest, what we think we don't deserve, what we don't give to ourselves, and therefore never receive the help we require.

I was overweight, and I had a ton of responsibility, but unlike the women in my neighborhood, I didn't ask for help. Even while paying for full-time care for two babies as I went back to work, I would still take at least one baby with me to the supermarket. No way was I an ungrateful prima donna who was going to leave her babies at home while schlepping a million bags of food for a family of four to her car through the snow! I didn't work hard enough for that, even though I was exhausted. So I ate. I ate because I was tired, I ate because I felt I didn't deserve better, I ate because I was guilty for not doing and being enough, I ate because I didn't measure up, I ate because I was overweight, and I ate because I ate.

The twins were a year old when we found out we were pregnant again—naturally, without IVF or any other medical assistance. It was the best news we could have gotten, and the best news for my state of mind. The hormones that were released during this pregnancy were making my mood lighter and lighter even though my body was getting heavier and heavier. I began to repeat all of the unhealthy habits I practiced while pregnant with the twins, and by the time I weighed in for my epidural, I was only two pounds less than when I was pregnant with two babies. But I didn't care. I was armed with the certainty that I would never allow myself to repeat falling into the same depths of despair I'd sunk into after the twins. The decision wasn't made as one of deserving; it was sheer terror that I would have to face the horror of living the same nightmare as I did after the twins. I had learned my lesson, and I was going to take the same event of having a baby and do it differently, co-creating a far better outcome with G-d's help.

I did the baby room in advance. I was now armed with the knowledge of how to go about it within the guidelines of the Jewish tradition. And even if I hadn't been, this was *pikuach nefesh*, "saving a life": mine! I was not going to survive what I had just gone through a second time, and in saving my own life, I would be able to be a much better mother to this new baby I hadn't even met yet. I brought both of the twins' stored baby clothes up from the basement and instructed the babysitter to only wash one of them as soon as we found out if we needed pink or blue. This taking charge and giving myself what I needed to feel like a whole person was so powerful that it prompted me to give myself the space and the grace to eat what I felt I needed during the six months that my new little Sophia was exclusively nursing. Because I had gone through the depression of what it felt like to not even be able to properly nourish the twins, no way was I putting myself in a position to repeat that because it was pure hell. I went out and bought myself clothes—real clothes that made me look like a put-together person. Even though they would be temporary clothes, I knew that if I looked good, I'd feel better. Additionally, after I gave birth, my hormone levels did a complete flip. I went from depressed to a state of absolute euphoria. With my old levels of energy and positive outlook restored, I was excited and determined to lose the weight I had gained. I was having the kind of experience I dreamed of having the first time around.

Before I returned to work, I had armed myself with another set of mix-and-match clothing from the Gap. I had two pairs of pants, one pair of jeans, and a few different shirts and sweaters that I could wear in endless combinations. There was a scale in the bathroom of one of the schools I worked in, and once a week I would hop on to weigh myself and keep myself in check. The weight came off slowly, but I was consistent, taking one step at a time. The cycle of giving to myself more and then feeling better for it continued. When I was more than halfway toward my goal, I finally went to a local diet center to help me make better choices and keep me accountable for the food I was putting in my mouth. I joined a gym that had a fabulous deal on personal training. I was serious about getting into great shape. And by the time Sophie turned two and a half, I was down to my goal weight. I hadn't been at that weight in years. I was thirty-seven, and I felt the best I'd ever felt in my life.

I remember going shopping for new clothing. It was so much fun I should have been arrested. And I splurged. I took myself to Madison Avenue during sale season and bought a Nicole Miller little black dress, a Dolce and Gabbana outfit for synagogue, a bikini, a waist-length bomber jacket from Armani, and a Burberry purse. I got some hand-me-down jeans, skirts, and tops from my slim friend Jessica up the block that she no longer had use for, and I was in business. I felt like a million bucks. Like a new person. I felt like Summer again, and I was on top of the world.

So here's the takeaway: If you're in a place where you're depriving yourself, know that there is a solution, although it may not be clear from where you currently stand. Whether you've had a baby or gone through some other ordeal in life that completely overtakes you, the key is to mitigate the damage by really watching and understanding what your habits are leading you to do, and then decide if it's time to break free of them and proceed in a different way. Know that you may have to fall down seven times—or more, as was the case with me—but if you keep getting up and watching for what you want and don't want in your life, the answer will come clear. It may take some time and some *chutzpah* to stop listening to the Dark Voice, but it will get clear. I went ten years with no kids, and when I finally had them, I decided to replace one pain with another by falling into my old binge and sprint habits. Much of my life continued in this way, as you read on in my story. But there is a choice, like the one I made after I had Sophie. You can allow life to unconsciously lead you in unhealthy cycles, or you can stop the pattern in its tracks and go against the grain.

In his book, *you²* (Texas: Pritchett LP, 2012), Price Pritchett reminds us that we can be like the fly on the windowsill that repeatedly catapults itself into the glass, trying desperately to escape until it creates its own demise, or you can back up and see that there is an opened door to fly out of a mere ten feet away. You can take charge and change your life story. My struggle doesn't end here with my babies, and my house, and emulating a "together" woman. Not by a longshot. Turns out I am someone who always strives for more, and therefore have more places to fail and succeed. And in going forward, I ultimately found my healing at rock bottom. My mountain was deep and high, and I had more digging to do.

CHAPTER 8

The Surrender Method

C hasing perfection is a funny thing. The ability for man to create the perfect life doesn't really exist, but if you believe it does, you run the risk of losing yourself in its pursuit and never end up moving forward. You just stay stuck in a hunt for something you will never find, and G-d will up the ante and keep sending you more difficult challenges until you surrender to the perfection He has already placed in your soul. My state of what I perceived as near perfection within a slim frame lasted for about a year until I gained weight once more. It was smooth sailing for a while, but life's winds were about to change in a monumental way, and my plan to "handle" it without the foundation of having resolved the issues that caused the bingeing to begin with would prove to be flimsy protection against the storms being sent my way.

In my quest to obtain perfection, I mistakenly looked to the gracious women in my neighborhood as an unreliable and elusive measuring stick, not understanding that they had many of the same insecurities as I did. They were just doing their thing, rolling with life, supporting their friends, getting through their days.

Like me, they had their ups and downs, strengths and weaknesses, at times feeling on top of the world, and at times feeling incredibly lonely. And while I clearly had much to learn from them, I mistakenly viewed their acceptance as a step toward perfection, and in comparing myself to them, I separated from them, sequestering myself in my cave of not-good-enough, fantasizing about how one day I would be set free. Whom do you compare yourself to? What group of people do you give magical qualities to and just assume that everything is perfect in their lives?

To this day, I have the utmost respect for these women, and only wish to portray them in the most beautiful way because they deserve it. But at some point they went from being role models to being a point of contention for me, which was self-created because I saw myself as less. In my mind's eye, I was still the chubby, unathletic Naomi chosen last for teams during recess in elementary school and wanted nothing more than a new proving ground for how worthy, deserving, and together I was. I was now a different person with a higher education, a career, a husband, a house, and three small children. I was ready to finally shut down the screaming that still rang in my head, reminding me to do more because I still wasn't enough. Another sprint queued up at the starting line, which inevitably would require its pre-emptive friend, the binge.

It started with logistics. The kids were getting bigger and the house was getting smaller. There was zero privacy. Alex once walked in on me while I was sitting on the toilet, watching Sophie play on the floor, brushing my teeth, arranging carpool on the phone, and putting Serena's hair into ponytails all at the same time. It was now completely impossible to walk into the front door without tripping over strollers and skates, balls and bats, coats and hats, book bags, and purses for five people. The castle we had bought for the two of us was quickly becoming akin to the old woman who lived in a shoe. We looked at upgrading to another home for a while but couldn't find anything in our price range. There was one house that I absolutely fell in love with, but it was $200K beyond our budget.

"Can't you do something quickly to bring in an extra two hundred thousand?" I asked Alex.

He thought for a minute. "Well, we do have twenty blue-eyed embryos in a freezer in a lab in Port Jefferson."

I stopped asking.

And then the recession of 2008 hit. It was our lucky break. Prices for labor and building materials were cut in half, but we were still a bit short.

Alex said we should go for it. "This is our chance. Prices will never be this low again."

"But we're still short," I protested.

"It's okay. We'll figure it out. It's now or never."

As I explicitly trust Alex as my running partner in life, we went for it. And in the process, a litany of unexpected circumstances would present themselves. As it turns out, building projects, kitchen remodeling, home expansions, and gut jobs were conversation starters in my community with other women who either had common ground with me, or could afford a much bigger, more expensive project. I was looking to some of those women as models to judge my own perfection, and I was overlooking the fact that they were just regular people.

I was sitting in synagogue one Sabbath and a friend of a friend of a friend who I always admired sat down next to me. She was one of those gracious women who could be spotted shopping on the avenue while perfectly coiffed on a random Tuesday afternoon, entertained exquisitely, had a perfect figure, was involved in charities of all sorts, and sat simply in her skin, owning her place in the world. In other words, a regular person who had different strengths than me but whom I saw as "out of my league." We exchanged smiles, and I immersed myself in my prayers and continued following the service.

"So, I hear you're doing your house," she whispered.

"Yes, I am!" I replied. "Are you?"

"Oh yes, I've been out every day with my decorator. I come home absolutely exhausted at the end of the day," she said with a giggle.

I nodded politely. I had a decorator, too, but I used my decorator in a harried two-hour time slot every other week to choose the necessities so I wouldn't spend a ton of money, only to discover cutting corners costs more in the long run. If only I could do the sheetrock myself and save some cash. But hiring a designer who schlepped you around all day felt so . . . glamorous. And impossible because I was at work all day.

We finished our prayers, and I felt the chasm between me and perfection widen. Here in G-d's house, I let Him slip from my hand.

The construction in my house was overwhelming. We could have rented a home like other people in my neighborhood did while the work was being done on their home, but that's not the Naomi way. We tough it out and spend that money elsewhere. I didn't consider peace of mind at all. Suffer and soldier on. There was dust and tools and two-by-fours and piles of sheetrock everywhere, and the truth was, I loved it . . . for a week. It smelled like change and fresh beginnings and the promise of something better. We all slept in the same room for a time, and we needed to put tarps over the beds in order not to get debris on the sheets. Then the conditions grew pretty gross. All of our clothing was in boxes and on portable racks and everything was dusty.

And then our kitchen got ripped out.

Because we were carefully watching our pennies in order to stay on budget as much as we possibly could, there was pizza until the temporary kitchen got set up. On our third night at the pizza shop, another put-together woman I recognized from the neighborhood came in with her kids. She gave me a smile.

"I knew you were doing your house," she said, "but I didn't know you were doing your kitchen as well."

"How did you know I was doing my kitchen?" I asked.

"Well, I've never seen you here at dinner time before, and with your figure, there's no way you eat here regularly."

I was stunned that she noticed.

"Back at you," I said with a knowing smile.

But I didn't know. I didn't really believe I was like her. But for that moment I created the hope and rode on it for a while. I was actually keeping it together as I saw the other gracious women do.

Until I wasn't. Cycle, rinse, and repeat.

My temporary kitchen was finally installed, but it was in the middle of the dining room and there was no stove. So, the trips to the pizza shop increased. The real damage caused by those frequent greasy dinners went conveniently unnoticed at first. All of my dry-clean-only clothes that were structured and fitted were stored away, and I was in lots of easy-to-wash Lycra. I was also in a money panic, so I increased the amount of private speech cases I took after my workday at school was over in order to supplement the cost of the construction. It was the beginning of my descent down the rabbit hole away from the ideal figure I had worked tirelessly to achieve.

I continued to be in contact with the perfect ladies as I bumped into them at the tile store or while shopping for plumbing supplies, or through the shared decorator. There was an element of being accepted into their wider circle that made me feel special. The more I interacted with them, the more comfortable I felt with food, my worth, and being in my own skin. I felt I deserved to become what these women represented to me.

I thought I was so close, dear reader. I believed I could make that leap and become one of those gracious ladies, but I had not yet found the Surrender Method. Let me explain: I created the Surrender Method based on the teachings of the founder of Hasidic Judaism, Rabbi Israel ben Eliezer, otherwise known as the *Baal Shem Tov*, which literally translates as "the bearer of a good name." Here are the steps:

1. **Submission:** While I could recognize that I was not alone creating my life as divine intervention and the Law of Attraction were always at work, I didn't believe I could surrender to it bringing me what I needed or what I could handle at different points in my life. Understanding submission to your Higher Power will strengthen your faith in yourself and in the power that supports you. Knowing that you are always co-creating rightfully takes the weight of the world from your shoulders and reminds you that you are never alone. One day you will take this glorious Submission to heart and just relax into your life with your body and food.

2. **Separation:** I had the power to completely separate from the Dark Voice in my head all along, but I had not allowed it to happen yet. I was separated *temporarily* (key word) from depression that was holding me back from my life's mission. If I could do it all again, I would have used that time in my temporary kitchen to be grateful and realize how lucky I was, and to meet new people in my neighborhood, and to create lasting friendships. Among other things, I would have treated my body with respect because I wanted to be healthy. A positive outlook and complementing action fixes most everything in life.

3. **Sweetness:** I don't mean a whole box of Snickers mini bars. I mean no more comparison, feelings of inadequacy, loss, lack, separation, having to go it alone, or fear of the greatness that the Universe has in store for us. Although we all go through difficult times in our lives, we get to define what they mean and the story we tell ourselves. Your challenges with food and anything else in your life can either be assigned the label "awful" or "exciting adventure." You can be "in a slump" or "on a journey." My friend Shanna taught me that your schedule can be labeled "busy" or "full." You can be "overwhelmed" or "productive." You get to decide the meaning you give it, which determines the sweetness in your journey, so choose wisely.

I had watched these women and believed them to be walking, talking, breathing public service announcements for self-love. I did not submit control to my higher power. I did not separate from the Dark Voice. And I did not live in the sweetness. I was living on borrowed time. I had forgotten I was Summer, complete and whole and unique, and my eyes were cast toward my illusion of perfection. In times of crisis, I folded to circumstance and the Dark Voice took over, and I fell victim to one of the Dark Voice's most destructive weapons: comparison.

In this case, the crisis was needing extra cash for the construction. My head was filled with negative, berating thoughts: *What are you thinking? You think you can be like those ladies? You think you deserve what they do? Who do you think you are? Only work is for you, so get to it! You eat what is cheapest! You don't deserve to waste time with self-care when you could be working! You're getting a house? That's enough! How selfish can you be? What kind of a spoiled brat are you that you think you can loaf around, expecting everything to come to you? Look at all you're receiving, and you want to take care of yourself? The unmitigated gall! Do something constructive!*

Although it was all still on a subconscious level, I listened obediently and put the last nail in the coffin of the ideal physique I had dreamed of. I discontinued funding my gym membership and put that money toward construction as well. And with that, the grace that I had begun to extend to myself was gone. The vast canyon of disparity between my current reality and the gracious ladies expanded until the parallels ceased to exist for that time. Gone was the Surrender Method. I uncomfortably began the cycle of sprinting toward work and filling out my stretchy clothes, and bingeing to comfort myself from withholding the self-care I deserved. All of this made me feel terrible, and I pushed aside the ideal I was so close to morphing into. Clearly, so much more was under the surface that needed to be uncovered and resolved before I could truly relax into my life in a gracious manner.

But here's the kicker: We would have been okay financially if I kept up the gym. I don't remember my exact finances at the time, but I probably didn't have to work that many after-school cases either. And we for sure could have spent more on healthier food. I'm not saying it would have been easy, especially in that haphazard kitchen. But if that was my priority, if I believed I deserved it, it for sure could have happened. What is your Dark Voice saying to you right now to undermine you becoming your best self? Dig deep, and remember that thought as we continue.

Later that week, I was in the shower after a long day. The shower has always been a time of evaluation for me. It's the only place I can really see how I'm doing—how well or poorly I'm dealing with life because it's always reflected in my body. Over the last year, the shower had been a time where I was happy and appreciated my toned muscles, and congratulated myself for all of the hard work I'd been doing. Because I'd been so busy with the renovations, I was just washing and leaving, but that night was the first time in a couple of months that I could take my time. As I passed the sponge over my arm to scrub off the dust that was all over my house, I immediately noticed that something was different. Very different. All of the beautiful muscle tone that was so prominent was no longer there. It was covered in a layer of nights at the pizzeria and money and time spent on lumber and windows instead of the gym. But then something very unexpected happened. My reaction wasn't one of regret or self-loathing as it usually would have been. My initial response was one of relief. *Oh good*, I thought. I stood there in a state of confusion. I had caught the response of the Dark Voice before my conscious brain had time to interfere and cover it up.

It would be years before I really understood how clearly I could hear the Dark Voice and how quickly and unquestioningly I carried out his bidding. It was too much to have my house done, and look and feel beautiful and healthy, and have my children and a husband. I believed the Dark Voice, accepted my fate, and fully surrendered to it without a fight. Something had to go, and I determined that my own body would be the sacrificial lamb. Giving up on myself was the courageous and noble move for the better of the greater cause. We must sacrifice for ultimate happiness! The "clarity" construed by the lying Dark Voice washed over me. I had been in the good for too long, and it was time to do some suffering. I cut myself to the chase and stripped myself of worth. Who did I think I was?

I was back to the comfort zone of deprivation. My very own living hell. That monkey on your back keeping you from what you are supposed to be, do, and have in your life. I had been running into the same brick wall of my (dis)comfort zone for my entire life. I was in another pendulum swing to the dark side, and I rationalized it away.

Do you feel yourself swinging away from having what you want in life? When you receive all the good things, does it feel so uncomfortable that you have to shake it up and get back to the dysfunctional and the bad? But G-d was not going to allow me to live under this fallacy for much longer. He was about to bump up the heat in order for me to open my eyes and see life for what it really was, and to fully recognize what really mattered. To see the Surrender Method in its full regalia.

My only reliable, free, and easily accessible solace through all this hell was running. I ran on and off throughout the construction and throughout my adult life. Running kept my weight down, and it allowed me to engage in one of my all-time favorite activities: moving. It was just me, the road, my choice of music, and my thoughts. And no matter my weight, my uniform—my running sneakers—always fit. It was a very forgiving sport.

I had gotten new sneakers, and my toes started tingling toward the end of my runs. I figured I'd just give myself time to wear them in, but as time went on, the tingling started earlier in my run, and I consistently returned home with some of my toes falling asleep. I didn't think much about it other than having to figure out time to get to the store for a different pair of sneakers, which was impossible if I wanted to catch the contractors after work and before they left my house for the day. That was, until I went to the doctor for a cold I couldn't kick.

"Anything else I can do for you today?" the doctor asked after prescribing medication to help my upper respiratory symptoms.

"Actually, now that you mention it, my toes keep falling asleep toward the end of my run."

His hand literally stopped moving mid-prescription writing as if he were suddenly cast under some crazy immobility spell.

"I mean, I got new sneakers, so I figured I'd just wear them in, but it doesn't seem to be working."

He finished writing the prescription and then handed me another one. "I want you to make an appointment with this neurologist immediately. Women your age who experience the symptoms you just described may have the beginning signs of—"

I can't even say what he said. I just don't even want to put it out into the Universe. G-d forbid a million times this should be true for any of us.

I left the office and immediately made an appointment with the neurologist for the next day. All of a sudden, catching the contractors didn't seem so important. Now, you would think that I would have been hysterical, especially with the urgency with which he expressed the need to see the neurologist, plus the crazy long pause. But deep down, what he suspected didn't resonate with me. My soul didn't recognize what he thought was possible for me, or belonged to me. There was this presence of what I would eventually recognize as the Recovery Voice inside of me, speaking out and finding its way to the surface through all of my monumental muck of chasing perfection. It tried to get my attention so I could reach deep, grab my faith, and have trust that this was not how it was going to go down. But the void was too deep, and the Dark Voice ran over that tiny Recovery Voice with a massive dump truck the instant I entered the MRI, and out went the Surrender Method with it. The Recovery Voice leads to the healing, not the Dark Voice, which was all I was equipped to listen to at the time.

As soon as I was immersed in the reality of the suffocating womb of the MRI, steeling myself with bravery while being assaulted by the series of jarringly loud, unnerving bangs, knocks, and buzzes, I panicked. I forgot that G-d ran the world, and wondered what would happen if something were really wrong, and what on earth my next move should be. I let go of G-d's hand, and in doing so, I forgot that He was holding me. Unlike the preceding months when I demonstrated the more subtle distrust in the Universe by forsaking my body for the sake of the construction, I started to sob uncontrollably as a massive wave of horrible worrisome thoughts exploded in my head. And, ironically, I started to pray with every fiber of my being and asked G-d with all my heart to please let me be okay. But there was no way this prayer could be of any help because it was a prayer to no end. Isn't it funny how we pray the hardest when we lose our faith?

G-d had tried to teach me a lesson during the construction and the subsequent comparison game I played with the gracious ladies, but I didn't get it, so He had to turn the volume up a notch. There was no choice but to go through the challenges and pray I would come out better on the other side. I was really hoping the lesson I learned would be a good one. I don't know about you, but I've been in the depression stage over my weight countless times, having lost and gained the same ten to forty pounds over and over again. I hit the crux of that depression in the MRI. *What if I die and this is it?* All those endless years of weight and self-worth struggle for what? The house was in construction shambles. I was never ever going to really be Summer. If you've indulged while out with friends, ate a whole bag of marshmallows in response to your condescending boss, or have completely fallen off the wagon after a period of being super careful with food, this is that depressed moment that comes after the misguided belief that you are in control of it all. I thought I was in control during the construction, and I thought I was in control in the MRI. You forget that you're not the only one running the show. Depression. Then food. You forget the Surrender Method of Submitting, Separating, and living in the Sweetness. It's the doubt born from the misconception that you were in absolute power when you created the first set of circumstances of getting yourself into shape, and then failed. We forget that the nature of life is that it ebbs and flows. Progress is never linear because we must experience setbacks so we can pick ourselves up, learn to be better, and then go forward valiantly. The Universe sets that all up so you can eventually become the person you were meant to be. All we need to do is dust ourselves off and wait in positive activity for the sun to shine again.

In the absence of faith, the same thoughts kept running through my head: *If I'm not dead, and my family can't collect my life insurance, and I'm laid up somewhere and can't collect my paycheck, what is my family going to do? Are my kids going to switch schools? Will they have to sell the house, and if so, will it even be worth anything in its current state? What's going to happen to my family?* As if I had control over any of it.

I was functioning under the illusion that I was working independently of my higher power, and that only I could save myself and my family. I was already using this exact same thought process that I did with keeping my family afloat during the construction, so it was easy to just add another incredibly heavy burden to my plate with this new medical scare. I kept having images in my mind of being pushed off a cliff, trying to catch one of the branches on the side of the mountain while freefalling so I wouldn't plummet to the bottomless gulf that awaited to swallow me whole. If you think that I separated from my soul during my earlier descriptions of bingeing on food, or you could imagine what went on in my temporary kitchen before the MRI was piled on top of it, you should have seen me now. I was the runaway train speeding down every track with the Dark Voice whispering in my ear, encouraging me to further spiral out of control. I carried out that bidding immediately. Food was my savior through it all, my right-hand man to steady me in the absence of the faith I could have so easily reached for instead.

And then I found out I was completely fine. Just like that.

"You're fine," said the specialist as he looked at me incredulously. "Nothing wrong with you. Get out of here and go home."

Now, I am a religious person, and a very happily married person, but I could have kissed that geriatric, unattractive doctor full on the mouth right then and there in that office. I did an about-face, bid him thank you and farewell, and practically floated all the way home.

It was a new lease on life. The sky looked bluer. I could smell flowers from miles away. There were rainbows on the sidewalks, bluebirds on my shoulders, and unicorns bearing gifts. The world was beautiful and hope sprang eternal. I ran home and never appreciated my family more. I was grateful for every leaky faucet, every unpaid bill, every one of the construction workers' tools that were left haphazardly in the middle of the floor, my disgusting temporary kitchen, my dusty, stretchy Lycra clothing, and every challenge I've ever had. I got down on my knees and reached out and grabbed G-d's hand once more, and there it was waiting for me, right where I left it.

I may not have had control over all of the circumstances that were thrown my way, but looking back it's pretty clear that I did have control over how I chose to react to those circumstances, how I viewed them, how I built them up in my mind, and the actions I took as a result. I could actually Submit to G-d and be better than okay. I could Separate from the Dark Voice and still be intuitive. I could live in the Sweetness and not have to suffer.

What if every time the Dark Voice told you something negative, you assigned it a different meaning? You would receive the stimuli from the Dark Voice, which would naturally evoke a certain emotion in you, but that doesn't mean you need to follow through with what it tells you to feel or do. You could decide that it's just a sign to be your best self. It's completely possible to remind yourself that the only reason the Dark Voice is appearing in your head is because you're getting close to the person you want to be in your life, so instead of listening to it, keep going in your current direction. But that takes conditioning, and I didn't know that. I had to learn it the hard way. We all deserve the sweetness, so stop spending your time needlessly chasing the perfection that already exists inside of you.

CHAPTER 9

I Got This

F ear of the unknown is the typical response when it comes to anything out of our control. When I had the MRI, I definitely felt fear and many thoughts of "what if" filled my mind. But isn't it amazing how confident and free of burden I felt after the MRI incident? Like that singular aha moment would finally set me free from the binge and sprint, the Dark Voice, and all the paradigms at play. As if I would see life for what it really was, get my priorities in order, and completely change the trajectory of my life. But that, surprisingly, didn't happen. I was not so quick on the uptake. I made all the promises and proclamations only to find myself a few months down the road worse off than before. The path to recovery from an addiction is never linear, and it is often the darkest before we step into the light.

While I was overwhelmingly grateful that everything was okay with my health, the idea of being on a financial tight rope sat like a stone in my stomach that was then shoved in my throat, and I was open for answers. That answer was quickly delivered when the business of network marketing was introduced into my life. My deep, heartfelt, true-blue intention was to take G-d's cue from the MRI and gently, with self-love and without binge and sprint, begin to slowly apply myself to building an additional business opportunity. Yet, in the absence of addressing the core wound of how binge and sprint was created in the first place, I reinvented the network marketing wheel and used this beautiful business as a platform to plummet myself into oblivion in an unprecedented way that was beyond confounding. To be clear, in no way did the industry of network marketing cause me to run myself into the ground. I did that all by myself. I was in an all-out sprint, almost willfully trying to annihilate myself. All the bad came roaring in with the good and the momentum my team and I were creating. Erratic food habits, avoidance tactics, and comparison fortified and directed by the Dark Voice through binge and sprint struck me blind to the root of it all.

One thing was certain for me: network marketing proved to be a place where my unresolved past showed up as I grew myself and my team. The beauty of that is that if you make the decision to deal with whatever is holding you back, you can shed it and rise to your potential. For me, network marketing was the ultimate catalyst in becoming the person I was meant to be on this earth.

My daughter's tutor, Becky, was a rep for a network marketing company and sold me skin care and makeup. She had asked me to join her business a couple of times, and it really took every ounce of restraint that I had in my body not to laugh in her face. Alex is a successful matrimonial attorney in Manhattan, and I personally command a six-figure income as a speech therapist. Why on earth I would want to sell lipstick was beyond me. No thank you very much. Despite the attractive compensation plan that could clearly benefit my family, it all seemed to be beneath me. Boy, was I ever wrong!

The day after my MRI, I was on my porch ordering an eye

cream from Becky on her way out after the lesson when the unexpected happened. She said, "I always just place your order. Are you sure you don't want to hear about my business?" Isn't timing just everything? Not only was I flying high with gratitude, not only was I on top of the world feeling that anything was possible, but I was in complete and utter "taking on" mode.

Have you ever had a close call in life and found yourself bargaining with G-d? "If this turns out okay, I promise I'll give more charity. Or feed the poor every weekend, or dress more modestly, or attend Mass every Sunday . . ." Fill in the blank. Well, for some unexplainable reason, I felt this pull that this business was the thing I was supposed to take on for having been given a new lease on life. This pull was so strong that it almost knocked me off my feet. There was no denying it, no ignoring it, and before I knew it, the following words were coming out of my mouth: "So, what do I have to do? Do I have to like, sell stuff or something?" Seriously, those were my exact words. Clearly, I had less of an understanding of what this business was about than a kindergartener would know what to do at a hedge fund. I had no idea what I was getting into, but it was clear—and I mean crystal clear with all the divinely inspired bells and whistles—that this was my path. And unlike my time in the MRI, I grabbed hold of G-d's hand and said, "Let's go."

I called Becky's upline, Sharon, early the next morning to give her my credit card to order some starter products.

"I need you to take my credit card right now because if I wait another minute I'm going to chicken out and not do this."

"Oh, sweetheart, I don't want you to feel pressured or rushed!"

"It's no rush. I've decided. I'm doing this. Take the card. Here's the number. Do you have a pen?"

"But maybe we can get togeth—"

"Take the number!"

That night I lay in bed with the worst case of buyer's remorse. I was panicked, sweating and freezing at the same time, looking up at the ceiling, completely unable to sleep. *What have I done? What's wrong with me?* I had a master's degree, several other certifications, and an acceptance for a full scholarship for a PhD to an Ivy League university that I was supposed to start in September. I was working a full-time job. So why had I decided to start a business that I knew nothing about? I started scheming a million different ways and coming up with just as many excuses to quit before I began and cancel my order for the starter package. I ran to the bathroom at least a dozen times. I was tossing and turning, jealous that my sleeping husband was experiencing the sheer bliss of being temporarily unconscious and unaware of my stupidity.

The room began to brighten with the dawn of a new day, and I sat up in bed with the rising of the sun. And while all of my fears did not fade with the night, one very practical thought crystalized in my head, fueled by our friends Grit and Stamina.

I whispered to myself, "Well, money's gone. Gotta make it back." Clearly, if I really wanted a refund, I could have gotten my money back. But what I really wanted so deep down inside that I didn't even realize it was another sprint. Another place to prove myself worthy. I had skin in the game in more ways than you can shake a stick at, and that alone threw me out from under the covers and into activity.

I started my business in true Naomi fashion with a tsunami of activity and a full-on sprint. I quickly learned about the company and the industry of network marketing as a whole, and I was blown away by what I read. I was that sure of where I was headed, and my instincts turned out to be right on target. I worked hard and built my business consistently by both selling health and wellness products and building a team of people that did the same, and after a time I found my team and myself on the cusp of completing the very top promotion.

While my perseverance and sheer determination continued to be the driving force behind the continued growth of my team and sales, the excitement and joy I found through my beautiful business had diminished considerably. It happened so slowly I didn't even realize that I had once again let go of G-d's hand and chained myself in the burdensome shackles of thinking I was the only one in control, and I felt that nauseating drop in my stomach with every dip in my team's bottom line. I forgot all about the first rule of the Surrender Method, Submission to G-d, and was in full control mode submitted to the Dark Voice instead. Binge and sprint governed my beautiful business, my happy place where the Universe worked so hard to lead me. What had I done?

As opposed to the flexibility that network marketing is so perfectly designed to offer the lives of its independent consultants, my business was all I could see and everything else in my life became secondary. I forgot about parent-teacher conferences. The house was a mess, aside from it being under construction. There was no way to keep up with the laundry. One morning the school bus came and there were no socks. It was easier for me to stop at the twenty-four-hour Target and pick up a three pack of panties on my way home from a late event than it was for me to put in a load of wash. Everybody in my house had forty pairs of underwear. But my business was growing by leaps and bounds. It was exciting and magical, and like nothing I had ever experienced before, and I didn't allow myself to rest, or celebrate the wins, or congratulate myself along the way. The only thing that existed was the finish line. Gone was the Sweetness.

When I first started my business, I did it by stepping out in faith. I was holding G-d's hand, and there was no question that He was holding mine. But somewhere along the way—when it was clear that things were getting "too good" or more than I deserved—I began to doubt being worthy of such joy, excitement, friendships, and momentum. I knew my new venture could be filled with all those things because I saw many others in my company doing it firsthand. Just like building the house, or being in school, or taking care of the twins, I was at that tipping point when the world was getting really good for me, but I was only "handling it." I turned the joy of pursuing my dreams into punishing work, and then I used food to steady me. Because if my business is doing well, the Dark Voice tells me that something else must be sacrificed, and we already know that's going to be me. But it wasn't just the food this time.

A full night's sleep was now a thing of the past. I was averaging between three and four hours of sleep a night, six nights a week, and then crashing on Friday night and sleeping through most of Saturday, the Sabbath where I had always enjoyed connecting back to my soul through spending time with my family, G-d, self-development through books and Bible study, and going to synagogue. I wouldn't allow myself to get to bed during the week until way past bedtime, convincing myself that there was still so much more to do when those things could have easily waited until daylight hours. I rushed daily from my day job to my business without taking time to enjoy the ride, or the wins, or the people. My routine of stopping at the gym on the way home from work came to a screeching halt. How could I allow myself time at the gym when I could be using that time to build my business? *Not making money when I could be making money is a sin! I mean, I am renovating a house! How irresponsible can I be? Madness!* My version of feeding myself was walking in the door with my coat on while still being on the phone from a conversation I had started in the car. I would grab whatever was laying on the counter. If it didn't have mold growing on it, or if it wasn't stapled to the counter, it was going in my mouth. There was pizza for dinner almost every weeknight.

When I was running on autopilot, how could I take time to be picky about what I was eating? There was work to be done, so what was the difference what I ate? I just filled myself, got it over with, and got back to work. There was no interrupting it. I had slipped from excitement and exhilaration into exhaustion and extremes. I wasn't guarding the gate, and my old habits slipped right through and took over. I gained thirty-five pounds . . . while selling health and wellness products! What a hoot! Well, if that doesn't beat all.

It was December 2013, the month that my team and I would earn the final and top promotion to the pinnacle of my company, that my body started telling me I needed to make a change. And I use the word *telling* lightly. That sucker was screaming bloody murder to stop, do not pass go, do not collect $200, hop on a treadmill, eat a salad, and get a good night's rest. In that order. I was driving home from a business event in upstate New York, about two hours from my home without traffic. The heart palpitations started again, but I ignored them as usual. I was sure they would go away like they always did, but this time they didn't. They were getting stronger and faster. I knew I could make it to urgent care right before they closed if I hurried, but that would mean losing another hour of sleep, and I still had to prepare all of my things for tomorrow and get to work for my first early morning patient. Not having time to get to the doctor was my excuse for not going when the palpitations first started, so that wasn't working. I reluctantly bit the bullet and pulled into urgent care.

The night receptionist didn't even take her eyes off her personal cell phone to look up at me. I wasn't even sure she knew I was there.

"Um, I'm here because I'm having heart palpitations."

Yup, she was looking up at me now.

Before I knew it, I was lying on a table hooked up to a bunch of electrodes, crying, imagining the worst, and wondering what was going to happen to my family if something was really wrong. It was the MRI all over again. I brought the same habits, the same patterns, the same mindset to sabotage yet another stage of my life that could have been so much more beautiful. And although all of that was going on, I was honestly just so happy to be lying down that I didn't even mind the cold stickies they were putting all over my body. All I remember was that poor technician trying so hard to keep me all covered and modest and doing his best to comfort me throughout the awkward procedure. Oy, poor thing. What a mess.

I was finished with the procedure and fully dressed when the doctor came into my examination room. I will never forget her, an angel sent to me straight from heaven. She sat down next to me, took my hand in hers, and asked me in her calming, soothing voice something I was not expecting. "When was the last time you had a full night's rest? Or sat down to a healthy meal?"

How did she know? Clearly, binge and sprint was now on the medical board examination.

"Friday," I said confidently and without hesitation. Two points for Sabbath!

"And before then?"

"Friday," I responded a bit more sheepishly this time.

She caught on. It was a Jewish neighborhood.

"Your heart is fine, my dear. You're giving yourself panic attacks. I promise that if you sleep regularly, eat healthy, and take care of yourself you will feel better almost immediately."

Well, if that wasn't a fine how-do-you-do! Panic attacks.

I didn't change anything.

Two weeks later on New Year's Eve, a few hours before the ball dropped, my team and I were pennies away from being promoted to the top level of our network marketing company. It was important because if you promote and meet certain qualification requirements prior to January 1, you can earn an incentive trip that you can attend with the guest of your choice along with all of the other top-income earners. Man alive, I didn't care if I had to stand in traffic on the FDR Drive in my underwear selling night cream in the freezing cold—I was finishing no matter what. And it's not that I could even conceive of earning that trip. I mean, could Mama use a vacay? Heck yeah! But then I thought, *I have nobody to watch my kids.* The Dark Voice told my soul that vacations weren't for me, and fun wasn't for me. I was the workhorse, and that was all I needed to concern myself with. No wonder I was unnecessarily running myself into the ground and couldn't find a way out.

So there I was, at home watching my numbers climb. I was sitting on my bed with my laptop and order forms flying in every direction. My whole team was calling me, appraising me of the orders they were putting in, wanting to know how many more orders we needed to promote. "Are we there yet?" It was a real team effort, and the excitement and momentum was through the roof. I got a call that someone had double-booked an event and asked if I could go and cover one of them in Brooklyn. I hopped into what was my network marketing uniform at the time (a.k.a., the only dress that fit me), told my family that I was going out to complete the promotion, and off I went. There were thirty-five people at that party, and by the time it was over, my team and I had earned our spot at the top level of the company. We did it. I couldn't believe it. We actually did it. I drove home along Ocean Parkway toward the Belt Parkway, and over the water I saw fireworks celebrating a new year while I blasted Chumbawamba singing, "I get knocked down, but I get up again" on the radio. It was perfect. Except for one thing: I was alone.

Clinically exhausted, overweight, out of shape, and utterly and completely alone.

I finally pulled into my driveway and ran into the house. "Mommy and her team earned the top promotion!"

Nobody moved. They were all half asleep having just watched the ball drop. They kissed me goodnight and went up to bed. I sat down on the couch, still in my coat because, honestly, it was so uncomfortable being in my own skin. I preferred hiding my body from myself under my coat for as long as possible.

I sat there in the dark by myself in my long winter puffer coat waiting to feel the exhilaration of conquering the goal my team and I had worked so hard for over the last few years. I mean, all those long nights with no sleep, hours away from my family, not taking care of myself... it was all worth it now, right? We got to the top. Goal met. Doubters proved wrong. Dreams vindicated. There should have been loud music and people pouring in my front door, champagne popping. At least my phone should have been blowing up. But all was quiet. Unlike me, everyone else was celebrating New Year's Eve in the warm embrace of family and friends. Even then, I instinctively felt the urge to turn on my computer to see what else I could do in furtherance of my vision. Always the workhorse. But it would have been to no avail. Aside from the fact that it was a holiday, I now had the arduous task of switching gears. My goal was met. I was hot on the binge-and-sprint trail, but I had no idea what I should be shooting for next, and I felt like I was floating with no direction. I knew I had to keep running. Looking back, I didn't know if I was running toward or away from something, but I knew I had to run, to sprint. And without taking a break or a breath, I kept going.

My saving grace was Sabbath, a twenty-five-hour period from sundown on Friday to sundown on Saturday dedicated to reconnecting to family, to myself, to community, and to G-d.

Now, I can clearly outwork anyone, but if G-d Himself took a day to rest, I could too. I would work with abandon until the moment I was required to light the candles, and as soon as I closed my eyes and said the prayer, I felt all of my relatives who have since passed standing near me in protection, and my entire body relaxed. I exhaled every worry, every stress, and every responsibility, and I got a twenty-five-hour leave from being a soldier in the army of the Dark Voice. I had always been a frequent entertainer, having several families to a meal at least every other week. Aside from connecting to community, having company is important because the more people you have in your home making blessings over the food, the more blessings there are to sanctify Sabbath. But I was so exhausted and short on time that entertaining became a thing of the past. I couldn't afford to expend energy in directions that I believed were not a dire necessity at that time.

There was one Friday afternoon where I scheduled a quick business meeting after my day job at school as a speech therapist. It was Friday, but it was May, and sundown was getting much later. I figured I'd have plenty of time, but as usual, I was running late. Super late. I was literally sweating as I pulled into my driveway. There was five minutes left until Sabbath. I hadn't cooked or even shopped for food. I hadn't even called home to let anyone know that I needed any help, big surprise there. I was shaking as I climbed the steps thinking what I could do in five minutes to create two acceptable Sabbath meals. I was picturing cereal for Friday night and canned tuna for Sabbath lunch. Did I even have challah bread or wine in the house to make the blessings over? Maybe after Alex left with Sammy to synagogue I could run down the block and ask if the neighbors had any extra. I couldn't believe I did this. I should have taken time to organize my home. Sabbath was the most important thing. I was responsible for creating a beautiful atmosphere on this day of the week for my family.

What would my children think? I was setting an example that this day was not important. Isn't there any way to make more hours in the day? I rang the bell. Footsteps. *Dear Lord, please let this be okay.*

Alex opened the door. Sammy was by his side. They were both in suits. I smelled food warming on the hot plate in the kitchen. The table was set. Alex looked at me with kind eyes.

"Everything is ready. You have a few minutes to wash up and change. Your candles are waiting for you to light them. I'm taking Sammy to synagogue, and I'll see you after. I love you. Everything is okay." He kissed me on the top of my head and off they went.

I didn't know how to feel. I was beyond grateful that Alex was so understanding, supportive, and proactive, but I was also embarrassed and disappointed for not living up to my responsibilities to myself, my family, and my covenant with G-d. I ran upstairs and teamed up with the Dark Voice to beat myself up with every condescending thought I could spew in my direction while I quickly got ready. I ran back downstairs, stood over my candles, and prayed a while, immersed in a pool of shame. I thought I was doing the right thing. I was working as hard as possible and sacrificing everything I could to work a full-time job and a full-time business so that I could provide in the best way I knew how. And what was the result of my full-week sprint to what was supposed to be the day of rest? Complete exhaustion that did not allow for even a semblance of what Sabbath was meant to be: a day of coming together with family, and myself, community, and G-d. Gone were the days where I had the strength to stay awake long enough to lounge at the table and play board games, hear about everyone's week, and exchange learnings from the Bible, let alone even begin to think of entertaining. It was becoming increasingly difficult to wake up early and make it to synagogue.

I could no longer keep my eyes open for the classes, study, and self-development I always practiced Sabbath afternoons.

Somewhere in the binge and sprint toward my ideal vision of the ultimate life for my family, everything went topsy-turvy and what I had been working for was lost in the pursuit. And although I didn't realize it at the time, my punishing work habits had nothing to do with what I was pursuing, or my job, or network marketing, or how many hours were in the day. My health and wellness network marketing company was all about self-care and a balanced life, the exact opposite of where I was taking my business. It all came down to me and trying to fill a void so huge that every boulder I heaved into it disseminated into tiny pebbles that took up no room at all. But I couldn't see it. Instead of doing the sane thing and ease up so I could get back to what fueled me and my business in a healthy and productive way, I focused only on the time I had already spent away from my family and all the concessions they made. I decided right then and there to step it up and make it happen in a big way. I felt the fire turn up a notch in my belly. It was go time. Game on.

CHAPTER 10

The Core Wound

I'm not going to lie. What's coming next is painful. Lots of conflict. Heap loads of conflict. Nothing blows open personal growth like conflict. My business, my job, my finances had conflict . . . so I ate. My living conditions were conflicted . . . and I ate. There was conflict from uninvited opinions and judgment . . . and I ate. My self-worth was at an all-time low, affecting my relationships . . . more conflict, more eating, and as a result, my outlook on life was affected. Conflict. Conflict. Conflict. Everywhere I turned there was something that would not let me rest.

Nothing worthwhile comes easy. In my culture, we talk about two entities called the *yetzer hara* and the *yetzer hatov*. *Yetzer hara* is man's inclination to do evil, and the *yetzer hatov* is man's inclination to do good. Think of them as the little devil and angel on your shoulders, whispering in your ears. All I was hearing was the bad inclination loud and clear. It wanted me to quit my beautiful business that I had worked so hard to build. The funny thing is that some of the reasons it was giving me made a lot of sense. "Come on, enough is enough. This is insane already. You're too tired." But then conversely, I heard the other excuses it was offering as nonsensical and I paused. No, not relaxed because that would be monumental . . . but paused. I stood outside the voice and watched it. "Quit. Drop this. What do you need it for? You're making a fool of yourself, and for what? Your husband is successful, and you make a beautiful living on your own. People think you're crazy. Focus on the house. You can spend more time with the decorator. Go get that new cookbook you wanted and try some new recipes! You haven't watched any of your shows in six months."

The job of the *yetzer hara* is to derail you. Literally. Think of yourself as a train on a track, heading full steam toward your destination. It will do anything to take you off your track. But regardless of how haphazardly I achieved the position I was in, that was the exact moment when I needed to be steadfast in staying on my track. To be the Little Engine that Could. If I had quit, everything I'd been through up until that point would have been for naught. Not to mention the fact that there were now a lot of people who were relying on me. It would have been like fixing up half a house and then burning it down. In order to live like royalty in that house, you first have to go through the burden of putting in enough time, effort, and hard work to get it done. I knew I was being challenged. I knew this was a component of the Recovery Voice that involved more than me. The Dark Voice could put me down all it wanted, yet I had some history now. Two health scares, three children, a home improvement project . . . I was stronger than I thought. G-d would not have put me on this exact path unless I already had everything inside of me to get the job done.

What we know to be happening and true is not enough unless we make the deeper change within. And I don't mean a dress size. Notice that I keep referencing this side-step to the actual emotional work. The turmoil I was attracting in my life started to reflect the conflict that was oozing inside of me. I was attracting it with others, inviting mayhem and havoc into my life until it was resolved. The Universe was delivering a crystal-clear message that I needed to come to terms with who I really was and why I possessed an inexhaustible, constant need to move, pivot, and be busy, or I was going to destroy all the good that I had toiled tirelessly to create. People would start to test me, argue with me, and otherwise conflict with me until I dealt with the depths of the core of my pain.

In his book *Nesivos Sholom*, (Jerusalem: Yeshiva Beth Abraham, 2001), the Slonimer Rebbe discusses in detail the idea that the only reason our eternal souls were sent to live on this Earth is to have the opportunity to do *tikun*, or "fix" our souls that are not yet complete. The Rebbe explains that after our days on this planet are done, and we ascend to the heavens and meet our Maker, the first thing He will ask us is, "What did you do to grow your soul?" And if you have no answer, you will be standing there with your mouth agape and nothing to say. A question is posed: Isn't it good enough to be a good person and perform good deeds all the days of your life? The answer is *no*. Since your soul is not yet fixed and whole, it has cracks in it. Therefore, your soul will not be able to hold those good deeds. They will fall through the cracks in your soul like a sieve. There is no avoiding it. If you are here on this Earth, the only choice is to forge ahead and break through your most painful challenges. Unfortunately, knowing this wise information is not the same as applying it. The Slomimer Rebbe never said it was going to be fun, but it's necessary.

My work with students as a speech and language pathologist had always served as a place of solace. Every morning when I entered any one of the several school buildings I worked in, I was free to shake off whatever clouds were following me. For the next several hours, I would be fully immersed in the beauty and innocence of the children I treated, and the camaraderie of fellow staff members. It was a bubble of tranquility that no outside storm could penetrate.

And then it happened. I invited the conflict in by commenting on a teaching method that was beyond my scope of practice. I believed with all my heart that my suggestion would only enhance the learning experience for all of the students in this teacher's classroom, but I should have just kept my big mouth shut. In less than a New York minute, I was ostracized by my peers in one particular school in the Bronx and became the target of bullying. Yup, school teachers who bully. Oh, the irony. My bubble of tranquility instantaneously transformed into a prison of conflict. I dragged myself into that school building two days a week with what seemed to be lead shoes. I would enter a room and the laughing would cease, and everyone would ignore me. I endured the silent treatment and demeaning stares by those whom I once shared meaningful relationships with. I ate lunch by myself. And dessert. And lots of snacks in an effort to drown my depression. I cried most days. It was a burden of unprecedented proportions that weighed like bricks on my soul.

It was at this school that I spearheaded a meal time program for students to expand the repertoire of foods they ate. One day, a student whom the parents and staff were particularly concerned about, had a breakthrough that would change the trajectory of her life. I was so excited, and I couldn't wait to share the good news with her classroom staff! As I walked the student back to her classroom, I heard an explosion of joy and chatter from down the hall. Someone had just told them the good news. But as I opened the door to the classroom, dead silence fell upon the room. It took me a minute to recover and find my voice.

"Hey, just walking your rock star student back to her class."

I skated across the proverbial ice on the floor of the room, made sure the student was safely back in her seat, then quickly left.

I lowered my head and hurried back to my empty office. Alone. I took a handful of goodies that were reserved for the students afternoon snack from the cabinet above the sink. I hoped nobody would notice they were missing, but honestly I was starting not to care. Why was it that I could help guide countless students to learn how to improve their intake of nutritious foods, and make gains in so many other areas where they had challenges, but I couldn't save myself? And even if I had said the question aloud, there was nobody to offer an answer. It was as if G-d was telling me I'd have to figure this one out on my own.

Conflict showed up all over my business in the blink of an eye, and I quickly found myself on the bottom of that dirt pit, governed by the Dark Voice. I knew I was the one inviting it in because whenever these issues arose, I was always a part of it, but I didn't know how to stop it. There was an endless array of bullying and distrust around me specifically. The scarcity and miserly mindset I was trickling down to my team kept us separated instead of working together to build to the epic proportions we believed were possible. There was finger-pointing, bad-mouthing, and negativity our businesses and our souls did *not* represent or stand for. I was plagued by comparison, and my self-worth was at an all-time low. I reached out for help, but there was no answer. Once again, it was as if G-d was telling me that I would have to figure this one out on my own. A stream of consultants that joined my team presented the same conflicts I had with my father. The number of consultants I sponsored who would progress in their business swiftly dwindled because, clearly, I wasn't being one of those types myself. No way to attract what you are not. I was rejected on all sides.

There was one referral from an old friend on the Brooklyn College swim team that I had been calling for a while, Abby. Abby kept saying that it wasn't the right time for her, but always gave me permission to follow up after a few months to see if perhaps her circumstances had changed. Her name came up on my list of calls for the day, and I was excited and hopeful to speak with her. She was always so kind, and we had developed a relationship chatting about our children, our businesses, and our lives in general.

"Hi, Abby, it's Naomi Joseph!"

"Oh hi, listen, I don't have much time to chat. Anything special on your mind?"

"Oh, too bad; I'd love to catch up. But, yes, as I'm sure you guessed, I'm calling to check in and see if perhaps now would be a better time in your life to explore starting your business."

"You know, my business partner, Julie is here and she'd actually love to speak with you about the compensation plan!" This is par for the course in network marketing. If a person who is considering the business for themselves isn't a "numbers person," they may trust someone who is close to them who is more "bottom line" to give them feedback on the financial earnings side of things. Clearly, Abby had spoken to Julie about joining my team, and she wanted a second opinion on the information I had already provided her with.

"Oh wow, fabulous! I'd love to meet her." I was so excited. Abby seemed incredible, and I was stoked about working with her.

Abby put Julie on the phone.

"Hi, so nice to meet you! My name is Naomi Joseph, and Abby's told me so much about you!"

"You stop talking and listen to me," Julie said. "We don't want your slimy business."

Huh?

"You think we need your business?" she continued, dripping with mockery of the highest degree. "Do you have any idea how much money our business currently makes?"

"No."

"We make so much it can make your head spin. Our business is far superior to yours. We don't need your products, and we don't need your business." Julie was yelling now.

I felt the wind totally knocked out of me. I was not prepared. I thought it was going to be a friendly call. My guard was down, and I was getting sucker punched. Hard.

"Don't you ever call Abby again, *do you hear me*?"

I took a minute to suck back the tears before I responded.

"I'm so sorry to have bothered you. It seems there was a misunderstanding. I'm so happy for all of your success. And I promise to never call Abby again. Have a good day."

My beautiful business that I grew, my happy place, became a place of rejection, low self-worth, and comparison where I was not measuring up by a long shot. A clear result of not dealing with my underlying issues. Even worse, I was allowing myself to be defined by my personal numbers, which were far from fabulous at the moment. I sunk deeper and deeper into a depression while the scale climbed higher and higher.

Then there was the conflict with the contractor. The abandoned construction zone. The contractor that we had hired specifically for the kitchen, a great referral from New Jersey, had raised his prices astronomically, and we would have to wait it out until our savings could cover it. My floors, windows, doors were already installed in the kitchen, but that was it. I had opened plastic shelving in place of cabinets that we eventually upgraded to metal because it got less dirty and it was "fancier." My old, mismatched, beat-up fridge and oven stood haphazardly, leaning to one side, and seemingly plunked down in the middle of nowhere. We bought industrial stainless-steel sinks with extended counters on either side, the kind you find in the back kitchens of low-budget burger joints. Buckets were used in place of drawers and my cutlery was constantly dusty as a result. It was a mess. The effect was complete sensory overload. There was no way to just relax for long enough in that environment to make a healthy food choice, and I was living proof of it. For example, my son, Sammy, is hands down the most respectful kid I've ever met, but even he was sufficiently disturbed by my altering appearance to say something. While eating dinner on a folding table and chairs in our haphazard kitchen one night with the rest of the kids, I noticed him looking at my expanding muffin top sprawled over my jeans.

"You're starting to look different," he said with embarrassment, his head bowed. It was like his mom was becoming a different person.

Even synagogue was dusted significantly with the residue of conflict. I would arrive late on Sabbath, unable to find anything that fit. One particular morning, after much effort and digging in the recesses of my closet, I managed to put together something decent to wear, but then noticed that the matching stockings had a run. I looked at the passing minutes on the clock, hoped nobody would notice, and bolted out the door. Once settled in synagogue I opened my prayer book and tensed every muscle in my body to hold back the tears, and then got upset that I was spending my time in synagogue wanting to cry. My house of worship was my one safe place left since my kitchen, my job, my business, and my mind—for the large majority of the time—were compromised at the moment. I was so angry that my sacred time in synagogue was being tainted by the conflict that followed me everywhere. I couldn't even escape to the Loehmann's parking lot anymore because they went bankrupt. I felt their pain. I opened my heart to G-d once again to make everything normal, but the answer wouldn't come in the form I was asking for. There was work I needed to do first, and G-d would not give in because the only way out was through. In my head I heard my father saying in his Germanic Yiddish, *Nischt kien brayrah*, "There is no choice." I had to keep going until I found the resolution to the underlying issue, the reason I was attracting all of the conflict into my life. And it was then that I suddenly stopped to catch my breath and a chill went down my spine.

My father? Why did I hear my father as the driving voice? I still didn't get it.

I was praying with all my heart when Sarah tapped me on the shoulder. I sit next to my beautiful cousin Sarah each week in synagogue. She's a clinical social worker by profession and by nature, and she is always there to lend meaningful insight. Just being in her presence makes me feel better. I felt so lucky in that moment to have her. My heart breathed a sigh of relief in anticipation of her words to me. I leaned toward her, my every cell waiting for the healing her words would certainly bring.

"You have a run in your stockings," she whispered.

"Thanks," I replied with disappointment. Clearly, had she known what was going on in my head, that conversation would have gone significantly differently. But one thing was for sure, it was becoming abundantly clear that G-d wanted me to figure this one out on my own.

Eventually, I didn't even make it to synagogue on Sabbath morning. Once, I woke up to the sounds of Alex getting ready. I opened my eyes and smiled at him and noticed something strange. He was taking his suit off instead of putting it on. I looked at the clock: 12:17 p.m. I'd slept through the whole thing. Turns out depression, exhaustion, and weight gain affects your sleeping patterns. I had missed my Sabbath morning solace in synagogue with G-d. And for what? For my internal conflicts that I could not yet fully identify, much less "fix." I felt robbed of my opportunity to connect to my soul in a deep and meaningful way. The conflict was getting more and more aggressive and was about to show up in more personal spaces.

It was a rainy Tuesday, and I was driving in bumper-to-bumper traffic along the Van Wyck from a professional development day in the city. I'd been waiting for my highlight appointment at this incredible salon in downtown Brooklyn for months, and I was so excited it was finally here. Late afternoon and evening appointments were difficult to come by because my colorist was so popular, and now the traffic in this rain was delaying me. *Hey, maybe I'm not the only one running late!* I thought. I quickly called the salon to make sure they would take me if I arrived after my appointment time.

"Hi! It's Naomi Joseph. I have a four o'clock with Kenny, but I'm running late. Will you still be able to take me?"

"Oh, actually Kenny's cancelled all of his appointments for this afternoon."

What? Why didn't they call me? I was so annoyed right then, but I kept calm.

We chose a date to reschedule. I wanted to yell at this poor woman, but I knew it wouldn't do any good.

"I was wondering . . . I rushed back from the city to make this appointment after waiting months for it only to find out that it's cancelled without warning. Would it be possible to perhaps apply a small discount to my next appointment?" It was worth a shot. Why not salvage what I could of the situation? Couldn't hurt to ask.

"Let me transfer you to the manager of the color department."

"Hello. This is Kenny!"

"Kenny . . . hi! It's Naomi," I said, surprised he'd answered. "I was actually looking for the manager of the color department."

"I am the manager of the color department."

This was getting awkward. Something deep inside yelled, *abort ship!* But I didn't listen.

"So, um, I heard you need to leave soon, and I was wondering if maybe on my next appointment—"

"My grandma is in the hospital!" Kenny cried out.

I immediately went into empathy mode. "Oh my goodness, Kenny! I'm so sorry! Listen, she's going to be *fine!* I'm sending thoughts and prayers for you and your grandma!"

"I have to go!"

He hung up. I felt just awful for him. I said a prayer for his poor grandma and kept driving, lost in thought, sending healing karma his way. The phone rang and I picked it up.

"Hello, this is Jennifer, the owner of the salon. What kind of monster are you?" she continued.

Huh?

"What kind of a pig calls Kenny and makes him cry?"

"Um . . . there must be some kind of misunderstanding."

"Yeah, there sure is. Someone who is so disgusting that they don't even understand how disgusting they are!"

"I'm sure—"

"Don't *ever* come into my salon *ever again!*"

Click.

Conflict. Sucker punched. Tears. Did I actually make Kenny cry? But how? I felt awful! I couldn't believe I caused him even more pain than what he was already dealing with. Not to sound totally self-absorbed, but I couldn't believe I'd been put into salon excommunication. Now I had no idea where to get my highlights done, and I was in sore need of a fresh "do." This had to stop. I reached out to ask G-d why this was happening, but the answer was crystalizing. He wanted me to figure this one out on my own. I spent the rest of the drive mentally combing the opened shelves in my kitchen and thinking what caloric mixture would make me feel better. And by the time I pulled into my driveway, I had a game plan. I entered the house and got to it.

I wish I could tell you exactly what I ate, but I never remember. It was all just a blur, standing there at the counter or the open fridge, still in my coat and hat and scarf, but basically I first attacked everything sweet I could find. Anything created in the likeness of cake or chocolate or bread or baked goods worked. Even stale, frozen hot dog buns weren't off limits. Then onto salty, cheese being my drug of choice. Next were combinations of sweet and salty, and smooth and crunchy. An hour later (yes, as I told you, bingeing is a total time suck) I was at the kitchen table, still in my outdoor winter gear, in a total food coma, numbed to the conflict, but not feeling any better about it at all. And with the addition of feeling disgusted with myself, I realized once again that G-d wanted me to figure this one out on my own. But that was the problem. I thought it was just me and the world, and that I'd have to reach for food instead of G-d. If I could just change up my mindset while searching for the solution in the midst of the worst epicenter of conflict, then radical change for the good would ensue.

You may be wondering how you can change your mindset, especially when you're in the thick of it all. Allow me to introduce the concept of death as it is related to the current situation. Death is the ultimate conflict because it is something that we don't want to face. Not only the death of our loved ones, but the death of the parts of ourselves that don't serve us anymore. How I handled food during loss was the game changer for me. I entered the other realm of understanding my codependence on food on a whole new level through an unexpected sudden death.

CHAPTER 11

Mother Knows Best

I received the call the minute after Sabbath ended. I knew something was terribly wrong because my father had never previously initiated a call to me, ever. He was of the old-world European belief that children call their parents, not the other way around. I held my breath as he delivered the news.

"Mother is in the hospital. She fell and hit her head. They asked me if I want to let her go. I told them to do whatever they needed to do to save her. And they gave me papers—I don't even know what they said—but I signed everything and they worked on her, and she had surgery and now she's resting comfortably."

Oy vey.

"Daddy, where are you now? Are you with her?"

"No, I'm home. I was tired. I needed to come home and rest. I couldn't be there anymore. I'll go back in the morning."

You have to understand, my mother was an eight-time cancer survivor. *Eight times* over a thirty-five-year period. In addition to that, she had surgeries on her elbow, her shoulder, her knees, and her heart among other things. Therefore I'm socialized very differently to the words *cancer, surgeries,* and *hospitals* than most people. To me, when my mother had an imminent, life-threatening illness or needed an operation, which was often, she went into the hospital, got whatever procedure she needed, came home, and got better. It was par for the course. So in my mind, this was just another one of my mother's "things." I couldn't even comprehend that there was something medical my mother had that couldn't be fixed.

I went to see my mother the next day, dressed to impress and coiffed in the manner she'd taught me through example. Her hair was always perfect, her makeup was always done, and jewelry complemented her meticulously matching outfit. I even brought flowers to cheer her up. But when I pulled back her curtain in the recovery ward, I did not see what I was expecting. I was frozen in place from the shock. There was my mother—my beautiful, perfectly manicured mother—with half her head shaved, and a row of metal staples from her forehead to the base of her neck. She had a tube coming out of her mouth that was hooked up to a respirator, and her chest filled and deflated at its command. There were monitors and wires and beeping and smells I did not recognize. I sat down next to her and held her bloated hand that was attached to an IV.

"Mommy?"

No answer. I was shaking. My head started to spin. This was real.

"Hi!" a peppy nurse said. She had come to change one of the nearly empty pouches that was attached to my mother's IV.

"Hi," I replied. "Can you please tell me what's happening with my mom?" She looked at me with the special brand of empathy that only nurses can deliver. They must teach that look in nursing school. I've seen it countless times throughout my mother's thirty-five-year career as a patient, and this nurse definitely got an A in that class.

"Why don't I get the doctor for you?" she offered.

This was not a good sign. My heart dropped into my stomach. The doctor appeared in under five minutes. Also not good. The doctor explained that given my mother's age, her condition, the extent of the hemorrhaging, and the size of the hematoma, there was no hope. She would not be able to continue to breathe without the vent, and there was no hope of her regaining consciousness. She was brain dead. My beautiful mother as I knew her was no longer.

I drove home in a fog and waited until 11:00 p.m., which was 6:00 a.m. in Israel and my sister Mimi would be up for her morning run. I explained everything as delicately as I could.

Twenty-four hours later, Mimi was by my side. She spent the days in the hospital as I went to work, but as the week neared its end, it was clear life-altering decisions would have to be made. This was more than a one-man job, and it was way too much for my eighty-five-year-old father to handle. We were it, the eighteen-hour-a-day crew. Mimi cancelled her return flight, and I took a leave of absence from work. The next week was an avalanche of conflicting advice, blame, confusion, guilt, and finger-pointing between neurology, general medicine, the oncologist, the advice from her vascular surgeon that needed to operate yesterday, respiratory therapy, the team from the vent unit, and palliative care, which deals with end-of-life choices. Mimi and I knew my mother's wishes because she told us point blank in her no-nonsense way with no holds barred. But we found ourselves in a tug of war with guilt and doubt from the conflicting advice that rained down on us from her vast treatment team. We turned to our spiritual leaders to guide us along this confusing and heart-wrenching path. They illuminated our decision-making, which aligned with our beliefs, and honored my mom's wishes so that she could be in peace.

So how did I fare with the binge eating through this? I'm about to let you in on a little-known Jewish secret. The *bikur cholim* room, "visiting the sick," is a kosher food oasis, or for me, a feeding frenzy for every stress, anxiety, conflict, fear, and latent childhood untended drama that could bubble up in the face of losing a parent. Designed with all good intentions to support and nurture stressed Kosher families like mine who don't have time to get meals, this room is located in several hospitals in large metropolitan areas.

I entered the room, hoping for some stale crackers, but what I saw was reminiscent of Willy Wonka's Chocolate Factory in all its splendor in living technicolor. There were individually pack-aged, thick, moist slices of chocolate babka, marble cake, and pound cake. Bagels and muffins. Sandwiches of every kind. A fridge filled with magical-tasting egg salad, tuna fish, cheeses, hummus, *tahini*, *matbucha*, *chatzilim*, and every spread you can imagine. And you should see what they bring for Sabbath! Gefilte fish and herring with horseradish. Hot chicken soup sat in a giant heating oven that looked like a fridge along with *cholent*, *kishke*, fried schnitzel, Yerushalmi kugel and potato kugel that delight the palate. And don't forget the fresh-baked challah. It was a veritable playground for the senses.

My mother was transferred from ICU to the Vent Unit, as the doctors had related at this point that there was no hope. It was conveniently located directly across from the *bikur cholim* room. I ate in there with wild abandon to steady myself because there was nothing else that was under my control. But as usual, the food served as an occupied distraction for only a moment prior to leaving me feeling increasingly and utterly exhausted.

From 6:00 a.m. to 10:30 p.m. Mimi and I sat, prayed, ate, were confused by doctors, visited with people, ate, sat, and ate some more. For two and a half weeks. Even though this was a dark and unknown time, I was truly in my element with so many decisions to be made all while growing more and more uncomfortable—if that was even possible—in my skin as I gained more weight.

Mimi and I had very different relationships with food. Yes, Mimi was always a foodie. She loves a good deli sandwich, eats hot dogs with fervor and appreciation, loves pasta, bakes like nobody's business, and doesn't hedge on tasting her creations. She will eat anything you put down in front of her with the exception of maybe tongue, but she knows when to stop. She's always been thin, with a frame to match, lithe with the elegant, long limbs of a ballet dancer. It was just her build, and her healthy relationship with food that allowed her to maintain it effortlessly. I, on the other hand, was always the "fat" sister, which was evident throughout our hospital ordeal. I was on a steady diet of Hasidic-supplied cake, and the sugar ran through my veins like a drug. I was hooked like never before. I wasn't even aware of how much I was eating. There were no windows in my mother's tiny cubicle in the Vent Unit, and it was as if we were lost in some strange space-time continuum. There was nothing to mark the passing of time but the shifting of the nursing staff. It was like some kind of bizzare magic trick when they left and then came back showered and refreshed when I couldn't even keep track of the time moving. Being on a healthy eating regime for me always meant keeping with the pace of the day. Starting with a healthy breakfast, eating lunch midday, and a small dinner at around six with healthy snacks in between. I fit them into my schedule. But there was none of that here. No schedule. No time.No consistency. And certainly nothing predictable. We were floating moment by moment. There was nothing in my control, least of all what I put in my mouth.

My mother also used food to soothe herself. When she was troubled, I would find her in the middle of the night at the kitchen table playing solitaire and having a snack. Like me, her weight went up and down, although she was much taller and carried it off better. We shared the same battle, and she spent most of her life on the heavier side of her natural state. Like me, she had unfinished business to tend to with her own Dark Voice.

If you don't have a healthy relationship with food in the first place, there is no way that one is going to magically appear during a crisis, especially not one of this magnitude. And it didn't help that the underlying root cause of why I binged in the first place still was not addressed. So, if you've ever lost your way with eating during a super stressful situation without a rock-solid, healthy foundation with food, don't feel too bad. It's a complete setup, and it's near impossible to win. The trick is to obtain that loving, relaxed, healthy feeling with food before the stress hits so you're already entrenched in some fabulous habits. If the loss hits and you are only a bit of the way there, don't be hard on yourself. It took me a lifetime to heal, and there I was in the depths of the binge.

My mom transitioned on a Monday morning. Mimi and my mom's sister Gladys had appropriate reactions of grief and cry-ing. But me? You guessed it . . . sprint. I was immediately in act-ivity getting the funeral together. Doing, sprinting, planning, accomplishing. Constructive use of every second masking a blind flailing in the darkness of grief, food was spiraling out of control. How else would I make it through the loss of my mother? That transition where I had to suddenly become accustomed to never physically being with her again in this life was, to this day, the most difficult test I've had to bear.

You don't have to lose someone close to you to understand what I learned from her departure. Because in some ways, death is like any other transition. The death of a relationship, the death of getting fired from a job, the death of leaving your home and needing to relocate. They are the most torturous mountains to climb, but the growth you experience when you come out on the other side is the stuff that makes us who we are. The challenge for me was not coming down the other side of the mountain three sizes bigger than when I first commenced the hike. What about you? Do you turn to food during times of loss? Do you use binge-ing like I did to navigate through your transitions?

I'm a big fan of Jewish burials. Not that I like burials, or the reason for them, but the rituals that are put in place are so meaningful. The tearing of the clothes of the immediate family members of the deceased. The specific prayers that are said, and the tunes in which they are recited. The way that the guests create an intimate aisle by forming two lines so they can recite the traditional condolence passage to the mourners as they walk through the center, away from the grave. But to me the most meaningful tradition is that Jews bury their own. Yes, the grave is dug when you arrive, but then the cemetery workers step back and the community takes over.

Six strong guests stepped forward and took hold of the straps that supported my mother's coffin. They maneuvered the plain pine box that held what was once my mother deep into the ground. Next, the rabbi asked us if it would be okay if she were buried with *shemot*. *Shemot* are documents or holy books that have the proper name of G-d written on them. One of the only permissible ways to dispose of them is to bury them. It was as if my mother had coordinated this practical organization of time and effort from above. Her stamp of efficiency was all over it. She had extended herself in the name of the Bible and her fellow man even now. No surprise there. After the service, it was time to fill in the grave. Each person took turns with the half a dozen available shovels.

It was the thud of that first mound of dirt hitting my mother's coffin that made it real. Before that moment, I was still caught up in the doing, mechanically going through the motions. But that sound of the falling dirt was so final. The sealing off of a lifetime. The cord-cutting of a lifeline. The termination of shared memories and future celebrations. The end of being able to pick up the phone and hear her voice.

I gripped that shovel and looked down into the grave at the plain pine box covered in *shemot* and the holy name and words of G-d. I asked my mom for her help that day at the cemetery. One last favor in addition to a lifetime of selflessly serving her family and her community.

"Please, Mommy," I whispered under my breath as the tears rolled down my cheeks and I threw the first shovelful of dirt into the grave. "Here's my doubt."

I picked up the next mound of dirt and let it slide off the shovel on top of her.

"Here's my low self-worth."

I kept going, shovel, after shovel, after shovel.

"Mommy, please. Take all this overeating. Take my fear. Take my scarcity. Take my not deserving. Take it all with you, Mommy. Please help me. Take it with you and bury it forever. I don't want it anymore. I miss you, Mommy. Take this all away from me. Please. I love you so much." I found in her spirit a partner in freeing me from my pain, and I knew that together we could do anything. I trusted her, and I trusted in her. I believed in my heart that she would help me, that she would always be watching and guiding me. I prayed that I was willing enough to accept her help.

Who has the strength for you, dear reader, when your pain gets too big? Because while mothers don't live forever, they never really die. There are so many souls that are watching you that are now pain-free on the other side with so much more strength and wisdom and time to guide and serve you than they could have ever had in this life. I had a beautiful relationship with my mother in life, but our relationship has been taken to an entirely new level since she passed. No joke, I feel her presence so strongly. If I'm going in a direction that's not right for me, I can actually feel her turning me the other way, and then giving me a kick in the pants down that road. Who ever said this has to be a solo act? There's no reason you need to do this alone. Call on your ancestors. They are waiting for you.

In the Jewish religion, we bury our dead as soon as possible, either the very same day of death or the day after. Once the burial is over, we mourn for a week. This period is called "sitting shiva," and while it is truly healing in so many ways, it is also yet another food extravaganza. Your only job during the seven days of shiva is to sit on a seat that is lower to the ground than others, wear your torn garment, and speak about the deceased. What their life was like, their highs and their lows, their accomplishments, the challenges they faced and overcame.

I was downstairs in my shiva chair by 8:00 a.m., spoke about my mom all day, which was cathartic beyond belief for me, until about 11:30 p.m. when the last visitor left. Then I collapsed into bed and did the same thing over again for a week. I was still suspended in the weird space-time continuum that started in the hospital.

During *shiva*, you are not allowed to shower—except to prepare for Sabbath, and even then there are some restrictions—put on makeup, or even look in a mirror. G-d only knows what I looked like. Well, G-d and the tons of visitors I had. Oh, and you're not allowed to prepare or serve yourself food. Here's how it usually works. One friend designates themselves as what I like to call the "head *shiva* monitor." My uber efficient bestie Rita assigned herself this role. Rita then called my other close friends and family, whom I will refer to as "regular *shiva* monitors." They then divide up who will be providing breakfast, lunch, and dinner for myself and my family. As people are so gracious as to volunteer their time, money, and effort, it is in poor taste to initiate meal requests. So, some nights you may get salmon with brown rice and a salad, or there can be endless days of pizza and baked ziti. On top of that, people randomly send platters. Platters of bagels with all the toppings. Platters of cookies and muffins. Platters of pastries. Platters of potato-filled *borekas* with hummus and *tahini*. The days are so busy with people coming in and out on their own schedules, and I was so grateful that they took the time to pay their condolences that I didn't even notice the passing time. Whenever there was a lull, the current shiva monitor would run into the room and yell, "There's nobody here! Come into the kitchen quickly and eat!" And eat I did. Whatever was put in front of me. Ask me what I ate all week, I couldn't tell you. But I know the majority of it wasn't healthy because at the end of that week I felt awful. I had a gluten headache that made the room spin, and my stomach tested the strength of my elastic waistband, threatening to break through it at any moment. In addition, if you have ever lost someone extremely close to you, you know that there is a physical aspect to the mourning process. There is this heavy feeling. A physical weight that you feel intensely with every movement. It's like walking around with a lead bodysuit on. Even the simple act of lifting your arm feels like climbing a mountain. There were so many variables pulling me down both physically and emotionally that I needed Alex to scrape me off the couch and put me into bed at night.

And then the dreaded Monday came and I needed to return to work. Don't get me wrong, I love my job, but going back to work seemed like deserting my mother. I had been in the cocoon of taking care of her and then mourning her. Leaving the house would mean separating from that schedule and, in turn, from her presence.

I cried to myself in the car on the way to work in one of the only skirts that fit me. I completely beat myself up for letting things get so far out of control. But looking back, I realize that when you have a history of relying on food to make you feel better, it's just about impossible to get control of food under those circumstances. I knew I wanted to be able to handle trauma one day in the future without turning to food, but just thinking about the strength it would take at that moment in time was exhausting. I could hardly exert enough pressure on the gas pedal to go but thirty miles per hour. I couldn't even fathom the amount of energy it would take to successfully make a life change that I had failed at since I was eight. Yet, the energy I had expended over the last forty years to binge and sprint, eat my feelings, and wage war with the Dark Voice was ironically far more tedious and exhausting than the Surrender Method of Submission, Separation, and Sweetness.

There is a Jewish law that during that first year of mourning a parent you are not to purchase and wear new clothing, listen to music, or attend social gatherings. On one hand, I was grateful for these laws because I felt protected from the pressures of needing to immediately emerge from the cocoon of the grieving process and become a functioning member of society. But new clothing, music, and social gatherings are all my personal joys and motivators. They pull me out of a funk. Dancing around at a party in a fabulous new dress to my favorite song? It doesn't get much better than that. In my normal life, if I received a party invitation, I would immediately shop for a new outfit, start watching my food, and hit the gym so I'd feel great when I was there and look as dynamite as possible in pictures. But during this year of mourning, I would receive an invitation, sadly reply "will not attend," and then eat six cookies in anticipation of another night on the couch in my stretchy pajamas.

Now, hold up! I'm not blaming my religion for packing on pounds. I'm totally owning up to the fact that I could have used the relative quiet of that year for deep introspection, or time at the gym, or spent that party money on a naturopath or a personal trainer. But the loss of my mother weighed too heavily on me. I was in a state of extreme lack and food was my go-to, my learned comfort of forty years beckoning to me. Not to mention that I had inherited another massive load onto my already-overflowing plate.

To add to this new twist of my reality, I was now my father's caretaker. An eight-year-old trapped in a fat girl's body looking like a disheveled overweight woman taking care of a mourning father. It was a recipe for disaster but also turned out to be the biggest blessing of all. It was what I believed at the time to be the final digging into the past. The final surrender. He still yelled . . . a lot, and all the time. If I sat through two and a half hours of traffic to visit my dad after a full day of work, he would yell at me for being late and worrying him. I braced myself every day for some barrage of yelling. But if I could look exactly one year into the future—the exact one-year anniversary of my mother's passing—I would be able to see the full extent of her meticulous planning in action. I would have seen how she left at the exact moment in time that would lead to me hitting rock bottom. And that in turn would lead to the exact time and provide the exact circumstances for me to begin to repair, or at least come to terms with, my relationship with my father and myself.

My mother's departure changed the narrative between my father and myself by taking herself out of the middle. It was now me directly facing my father and what I grew up thinking I should or shouldn't do. My agency and authority over myself had been warped so I created the binge and sprint to survive. My mother apparently had far more ways to help me now . . . sitting next to G-d up in Heaven, giving Him some help to guide my healing.

CHAPTER 12

Dealing with Dad

W live, and often suffer, in a false truth that was created long ago. A truth that was originally instilled in us by our parents, teachers, coaches, religious leaders, older siblings, and family members, or the big schoolyard bully during our formative years. So we accept that truth as our reality and our identity. Children are really great observers, but due to their young development, they are limited in interpreting the real meaning behind the messages. They take what others say as gospel and permanently emblaze it on their own chests forever, good or bad, like the Scarlet A. And then, like a snowball rolling downhill, it gains heft, weight, and density as it picks up the material around it. In his theory of relativity, Albert Einstein teaches that "Everything is energy and that's all there is to it. Match the frequency of the reality you want, and you cannot help but get that reality. It can be no other way." We can change the energy of the trauma in our bodies by creating a new story and truth, aligning only with the new matching emotion and beliefs, and participating in the corresponding actions. You think you don't have a choice, but I am here to tell you that you absolutely do. Each of us carries baggage that potentially blocks us from allowing our best lives to be attained. Some people operate in "victim mode" and are constantly fighting to get out from under layers of burden, heaviness, disappointment, and lack. Some people are afraid and avoid conflict at all costs. Others put up walls and attack to protect what is theirs. They are in "reaction mode" and get what they want by coercion because they are terrified that something meaningful will be taken from them. Turns out that these instincts—originally instilled in childhood—never leave you completely.

Are you operating your life from the false truths of your past? Are you truly aligned with the core essence of who you are? Examine your habits, addictions, co-dependencies, or self-sabotaging behaviors. Food and my false truth of not being good enough runs through my whole life. I topped it off with big-time overachieving at all costs. I did not feel worthy enough, or give myself permission to completely relax into myself as I am. With the discomfort of my shame that I should be doing something more worthy with my life, or be more organized, or prettier, or smarter, or just better on a million different levels, I hid in the kitchen and binged on cookies dipped in chocolate sauce because *that* is a guarantee I will feel *not* better. That allows me to stay in my state of not-good-enough, which is what the Dark Voice tells me to do. But at the same time, bingeing allows me to temporarily leave the painful state of "should" because bingeing fills the criteria of being busy with something, yet I am never out of "should" because it is the story I carry around from childhood. But the silver lining—the saving grace of it all—was that the inability to take hold of myself at that time was the exact catalyst that attracted the beginnings of the final lessons I needed to make a change forever. I needed it, and G-d sent it.

That year after my mother passed, my father plundered me with "should" every day of the week in my most vulnerable state. No matter what I did, there was nothing I could do to make him happy. I was never good enough, I never did enough, and I couldn't eat enough to make myself feel better, and I know that because I binged as hard as I could but to no avail. Was I capable of understanding and dealing with what he was going through after losing his wife of sixty years? Not a shot in Hell. Instead, we yelled at each other with every encounter through our shared grief over our insurmountable loss. The past became present in vivid, living color with even more special effects than I could have conjured from memory.

One of my favorite quotes is by Winston Churchill: "If you're going through Hell, keep going." Even the Lubavitcher Rebbe often stated that the reason Moses came down with the Ten Commandments in the desert is because the desert signifies death where nothing can grow. Yet from the commandments that were brought forth in that very desolation, we can grow to the highest of the highs. There's a great quote going around Instagram that says, "That setback gonna hurt, but that comeback gonna be a beast!" Now, I'm not saying it's fun when you're going through the setback part! So if you're going through a rough time right now and not "feeling it," that's completely understandable, and you're in good company. It happens again and again in life that when you've taken all you can possibly bear, the glimmer of salvation begins to dawn. But not a moment before.

It was exactly one year after my mother passed away and I was bingeing and sprinting off the charts. I needed Presidents' Week off from work for *me*. The constant input of bad food only served to intensify my feelings of exhaustion and made it increasingly difficult to pull myself out of bed each morning before sprinting to my full-time job, my business, my trips back and forth from my dad on Staten Island, the twins' college applications, household duties, and so many other things I don't want to bore you with.

I had caved and finally bought new clothing to fit my expanding frame in an effort to feel a bit more human. And although they saved me the humiliation of having to search endlessly to find a decent outfit each morning, they were beginning to get tight. The once-loose waistbands on my jeans were now cutting into my stomach, the breadth of which my body had never seen while not pregnant. It gave me a muffin top that could be seen through my new shirts that were so carefully chosen to mask just that issue. I hardly recognized my reflection in the mirror. The angles of my face were softened and enlarged, and blended into one another so that all definition was lost. My eyes and nose were drowning in a sea of flesh, and I did not look like the person I once was. It seemed as though everything about myself had changed. My mood. My reflection in the mirror. My attitude. My outlook on life. I was too exhausted to fully engage in my business, my job, my family, my community, my friends, my religion. I was just going through the motions and allowing life to lead me instead of being the grab-the-bull-by-the-horns person I was my entire life. I went from "get up and go" to "flatline on the couch." It was a drastic, life-altering, marked change, and I felt completely devoid inside of the person I once was. I needed that week to regroup. Get to the gym every morning. Food-prep leisurely. Get to bed early. Ample time for building my business. Read. *Relax* (maybe). During this time, Sabbath was the only thing that kept me connected with G-d and His presence as He held me in His hand. A day where my only job was for introspection and praying for a better tomorrow.

That Friday before Presidents' Week at school dragged in anticipation of a full nine days to myself. Alex was going to work, and my kids had school. I was salivating at the thought of having this much-needed time to get myself together. Like, foaming at the mouth and actual drool running down my chin. The final bell rang. I practically skipped out of the building and sang my goodbyes to my fellow staff members. I got in the car, blasted the radio since my year of mourning was just over, and drove the five minutes to the gym with a smile so big that it looked like I had a hanger in my mouth. I parked, shut off the motor, and was about to grab my gym bag when my cell phone rang. It was Roberta, my dad's cousin from Chicago. I reasoned that she must be calling to wish me a Good Sabbath.

"Hi, Roberta!"

"Hey, I'm so glad I caught you. Have you spoken to your dad recently?"

"Yeah. We spoke Wednesday. I was going to call yesterday, but I got home too late. I was going to call today before Sabbath." The truth was that we had yelled at each other so much that I couldn't bring myself to call yesterday. I instantly felt ashamed that I didn't.

"Naomi, I just spoke to him and he doesn't sound good. I mean, he sounds . . . off. I've never heard him like this. Maybe give him a call and see what you think? He may need to get checked out."

Now I felt really terrified. Terrified and terrible for not being more on top of his care. My eyes swung to the gym. Almost free . . .

"Naomi, I hope it's okay that I said something to you."

"Roberta, of course! *Thank you* for being in touch with him! Thank you for caring and letting me know. It takes a village." A village indeed, especially since I was clearly not doing my job. I was nauseated with guilt.

I immediately called my dad. He did sound different. Nothing alarming, but different. He said he was fine, just tired. But he wasn't as sharp as usual. I looked at the clock. The sun was setting early, and there was no way I'd make it to Staten Island before sundown. There wasn't even time for me to work out and shower. All good, I'd have the whole week. There was even a spin class right after Sabbath. I wished him a Good Sabbath, and used the remaining time to call my sister Sarah. Sarah said she was going to my dad's tonight and tomorrow afternoon and would see what was up. Sarah usually went Friday night to light candles with him and enjoy all of the rituals of Friday night dinner, and I was grateful to Sarah for hanging out with him on a regular basis.

I peeled out of the gym parking lot and made it home just in time to put up hot water, warm the food, set the lights, do some last-minute cleaning, and take a five-minute shower before sundown. I lit my candles and thanked G-d for Sarah being there for my dad, for my entire week off, and for this day of rest. I said the blessing over the candles, felt my mom's presence along with so many that came before her, and melted under G-d's protective wing. I was at peace, if only for twenty-five hours.

In this state of temporary relaxation, I reflected on the fact that I was now my father's caretaker. I thought about all the times my father took care of me when I was sick. When I was growing up, being sick was the best, most relaxed time. You're sick! You have to rest and relax! All bets are off. You have to spend the day in bed. I was applauded for sleeping late. I didn't have to do anything constructive. It was the only time in my life that I earned a full pass to just relax. I could lay in my pajamas and watch television all day out in the open without fear that anyone was going to tell me to get busy and move. And of all people, my dad loved to take care of me! He would buy me coloring books and my absolute favorite, connect the dots, accompanied by a brand-new box of crayons. He would sit on the edge of my bed and read me any story I wanted. He had the patience to watch while I put on a show for him with my stuffed animals and listen as I went on about my day, and he even told me about his. He would personally put on the vaporizer in my room and give me my medicine and help me apply Vicks VapoRub to make sure it was done just right. To this day, the smell of Vicks VapoRub gives me that relaxed feeling. And now it was my turn to care for him. Role reversal indeed.

Sarah called the second Sabbath was over, and she sounded worried. Daddy wasn't himself. He wasn't as lucid and his movements seemed a bit slower.

"He was fine, just . . . different," she said. As he was already asleep for the night, we planned to meet at my dad's house and take him to the hospital the next morning. I hung up the phone and realized too late that I had already missed half the Saturday night spin class. *All good,* I thought to myself. *I'll go straight to the gym after I get back from the hospital tomorrow. Plus, I have the entire week!*

The next morning, Sarah walked my dad into the emergency room and got him settled in the waiting room while I parked the car. She had so much patience. Looking at her help my dad off with his coat while I waited in line to register him at the front desk brought back memories of her sitting by my mom's bedside in the hospital while Mimi and I spoke to doctors about a plan of action. Sarah would sing and read poems to my mom and bring peace to an otherwise chaotic and disturbing situation. We each went to our strengths, and I was overwhelmingly grateful for hers at this moment because I myself was on the brink of a complete meltdown. I was playing a continual game of leap and hope, bingeing and then pushing myself as hard as I could in the sprint, praying it would all magically work out. But through it all, I had never allowed myself to be frail. That was not allowed. There was no excuse for that type of weak behavior. Bypass fragile and frail and go right into meltdown, and the meltdown would be imminent. Stick a fork in me, I was *done.*

My dad was assigned a spot in the hallway on a gurney in the overcrowded emergency room. A physician's assistant assessed him to see if he was oriented to person, place, and time.

"Mr. Brenner, who is the vice president?"

Pause.

"Why? He doesn't do anything anyway."

Good cover.

"What day of the week is it?" Okay, for sure he would get this one! It was Sabbath yesterday, the day our entire lives revolve around. He's got this! Or not.

And then it happened. Helpful, well-intentioned Sarah opened her mouth to give our father a hint after an awkward pause, indicating he would once again not be able to answer the question. Just to jog his memory a little bit so he would feel more in control. But to my father, it was pandering and belittling, and the end result was not good. Nobody could have anticipated his shocking, condescending attack in response. His words rendered everyone within earshot speechless, silent, and still. I looked at Sarah and saw my own familiar expression of shame and low self-worth painfully imprinted on her face. *I feel your pain, sister.*

"I'm assuming that his outburst is only consistent with these new symptoms that he's displaying. Not like he does that on a regular basis, right?" asked the PA.

Sarah and I looked at each other and then dead-panned the PA. "Nope, that's how he usually acts."

The PA stood there with her mouth agape for a full five seconds. "Um, okay then. I'll be back with the results after the tests are completed."

We watched her walk away, feeling slightly better and sadder at the same time, at the apparent validation of our feelings.

I didn't get home that night, or any night, for the remainder of that week until after eleven, and I arrived at the hospital by eight each morning to catch the doctors on rounds. So much for the self-care I had planned. I spent my coveted week off speaking to doctors, responding to my father's requests, and of course frequenting the *Bikur Cholim* room. The decadent treasures hidden inside remained both a blessing and curse.

It was on my way back up to my father's floor from one of these trips that I heard yelling. The loud yelling did not sound familiar, but I had a sinking feeling that my dad was the cause of it. My dad's roommate was about thirty years younger than him, at least six-four, extremely broad, and hands down the scariest looking man on Staten Island. He was standing at the nurse's station with his tube socks pulled all the way up to his knees and two standard-issue hospital gowns—one on his front and one on his back to cover his breadth—that came only to his mid-thigh, and he was hooked up to an IV, but none of that in any way diminished the terror and reverence his countenance invoked.

"Nurse!" he bellowed in a tidal wave of a voice that reverberated off the walls and practically shook the entire hospital. "I want my room switched. *Now*. That guy is *pissing me off*!" He pointed an accusing finger coming out of a large fist the size of a melon to where my father was standing, looking as innocent as a sacrificial lamb. He was leaning on a walker, in matching outfits with his roommate, although my father's gown almost touched the floor. He shrugged his shoulders, held his palms face up, and opened his blue eyes wide with confusion.

"All I did was ask him to turn his television down," my father said in disbelief, successfully making his accuser seem over-reactive.

But I knew better.

"That is *not* what you said, mister!"

This was going to be good.

"I was just trying to offer a helpful suggestion for your benefit," my father offered in a completely altruistic, heartfelt manner.

Wait for it, wait for it . . .

"By saying that what is wrong with society as a whole is that people like me watch television and get stupid and don't achieve anything."

My dad knew the gig was up and had no more patience for the charade. "Ah, come on already! You've had that *fakakta* television on all day and all night! How is anybody supposed to get any rest around here?"

"I like the white noise. It helps me sleep!" said the roommate, defending his point.

"*Gey avek!* Hey, nurse, I second the motion to get him outta my room. And good riddance with your *fakakta* television." And with that, my father turned around his walker and shuffled back into his room.

And while I watched my father disappear through the doorframe, practically dragging the tail end of the hospital gown on the floor, I was frozen in place, jaw hanging open, and I could hardly breathe as the full-body impact of the truth was suddenly hurled at me with the force of a falling asteroid. *His screaming was for everyone . . . not just me.* Which meant that he wasn't harder on me than he was on anyone else, least of all himself. And clearly he didn't hold back letting everyone know his point of view. Even if it put him in the way of bodily harm. Even if it hurt the people he loved because he thought it was the right way to live. I don't know why I hadn't understood this before, but with my mom no longer being my protector, I saw his pain. I saw I wasn't more bad, or wrong, or less than anyone else in his eyes. Maybe it was all his perception and how he saw the world from how he grew up in the war years. His own Dark Voice, and who he authentically became in turn.

And then I had a second thought, and this thought was pretty disturbing. But I'm going to be honest with you just in case you've ever had a similar experience so you don't feel all alone, so please don't judge me. All along I thought my father had "chosen" me to scream at the hardest because I was unique, and I used that to make me feel superior in some weird, twisted way. But if those outbursts weren't saved just for me, then what makes me special now? Clearly, I wasn't doing anything good enough that was special, and now it was clear that I didn't screw up bad enough to be yelled at any more than anyone else either. I felt as if I was floating after someone had untied my anchor and the radio I used to contact the Coast Guard was busted. The screaming had *nothing to do with me*. That's why nothing I could do would ever make him happy. The reality of my powerlessness in the exact space where I had binged and sprinted my whole life to make things right with my father was overwhelming. The hallway began to spin. It was as if someone had ripped the identity out from my soul and tossed it in the air like confetti for the wind to blow every which way. I couldn't breathe. But I was soon brought back to my current reality. There was work to be done. Things to do and accomplish. I was in the middle of a hospital crisis, for goodness' sake! How dare I take time for introspection at a time like this! What was I thinking? How selfish could I be? I shook it off, stuffed the feelings down, and chose to ignore them for the time being. Time to get back to work.

I understood then that I internalized my father's actions in a way that distressed me, and that became my story. But just because I had this realization doesn't mean the underlying damage—the thought processes, reactions, and habits the damage caused—easily went away. What stories are you telling yourself that are no longer serving you and are holding you back? And if you are past that point and have had a breakthrough, but you're still stuck in the muck of it, be kind to yourself. It took a long time to get there, and it may take a long time to undo. Hang in and keep going.

There is a commentary in the book of Numbers in the Bible, when the Jews were traveling through the desert, that says: "G-d isn't as clear when you travel," meaning that as you journey through life and learn new concepts, it takes a while before you can understand them on a physical level and incorporate them into your life. The truth about aha moments is that they are not a burst of brain synapses that make all the dots suddenly connect. You are not struck with a bolt of lightning that immediately gives you closure and healing. Contrary to popular belief, aha moments are not a straightforward path for change and freedom from old thought processes. Aha moments are actually divided into two categories: euphoric moments and roller coaster moments. The euphoric moments are powerful and instantaneously life-altering. The roller coaster moments are more of those sudden downward drops where you think your stomach is going to bottom out from your new realization, and you are left physically and mentally depleted. You will therefore not be able to apply the roller coaster lessons in the moment or anytime soon after learning them. So, take yourself off the hook and don't beat yourself up over it if it takes you a while to incorporate them into your daily thought repertoire. You're doing fine, just give yourself some grace. Taking time to recover from the shock of the new awareness, the death of the old thoughts, and the application of the new patterns, was the case with me as I hardly had any time to fully wrap my head around my new awareness of what made my dad tick.

My non-holiday week was over, work was starting, and I still needed to get my dad settled into rehab. That's when my son Sammy found me catatonic on the couch at twilight watching *Shtisel* in the dark. None of my kids had ever seen me not moving before. Lying on the couch under the covers with the lights off at 6:00 p.m. on a weekday watching television was something they had never seen me do. So, it was understandable when Sammy stood there watching me like a deer caught in the headlights wondering what was going on.

"Um...Mom?"

"Yes, baby."

Pause.

"Are you okay?"

"Yes."

Pause. Looking around for help.

"Are you sure?"

"Yup."

Pause.

"Can I get you anything?"

"Nope."

Pause.

"Do you need me to call anyone? Dad? Um . . . maybe the doctor?"

"Nope."

Pause.

"Are you sure you're okay?"

"Yeah, I'm just resting."

"Okay. Maybe I'll check back on you in a little while."

"Good idea."

My family was always there to support me, but I never gave them many opportunities to do so because I was too busy moving to express my grief. How were they to know? I never allowed them to see under the façade, until now, so this was a first for them. I knew it was bad if not even the Dark Voice could throw me off the couch and into activity. At that moment, not even a whole box of Cap'n Crunch could make me feel worthy, or accomplished, or enough.

The meltdown had commenced. Once again, Mimi flew in to save me. I handed the torch to her, she picked up with our dad where I left off, and I collapsed to recuperate on the couch. I was sick with emotional exhaustion, physical exhaustion, in all the trappings of being the heaviest I've ever been. And I'm telling you, that week of complete *surrender* lying there on the couch, tending to my wounds and excusing myself from every responsibility, was the most relaxed I had ever been in my life. There on the couch, with these memories colliding with the complete collapse of every maneuver and ploy to keep sprinting, a new story was emerging . . . but I was out of fight. While in the past there had always been rebound and recover, I felt this time was different. To survive this passage, I had to call out the depths of my pain and ask for help.

CHAPTER 13

Getting Help and Support

My very first attempt in getting professional help was in college when I went to see a social worker from the approved insurance list. He was the first person I ever told my story to, and in the midst of pouring out my heart with tears streaming down my face, he interrupted me mid-sentence and said, "Time's up, see you next week." I didn't go back. In fact, I made the mistake of not seeking help again for the next twenty-five years. Therapists are just people, and finding a therapist that is right for you is often like dating. Just because someone may not be a match for you, don't throw out the baby with the bathwater and stop looking. It turned out I needed to kiss a couple of frogs before meeting my personal Prince Charming of therapy, but he was out there! If you think therapy is what would help you, don't let the first one scare you off. Keep going until you find your match!

The next time I went to therapy, I was in the throes of the busiest time of my adult life, with three small kids and working more than one job. That bout of therapy sessions lasted six weeks. I did not allow myself the luxury of self-care. Neither attempt was effective or helpful, and at the time I thought therapy was insignificant.

I did not revisit the notion of therapy until a dear friend referred me to Dr. Ira Sacker a few years prior to my mom's passing. I went into our first session in true Naomi fashion, on a goal-oriented mission. I wanted to know how many sessions we would need, and what a realistic end date would be. I wanted to pencil it in my calendar. Looking back, I'm giggling at my naiveté because Dr. Sacker and I worked together for years, and still do. I have a lot to unravel. In fact, I met with Dr. Sacker for one of my regularly scheduled sessions the very week of my aha moment with my dad in the hospital.

When I walked into his office, distraught and the heaviest I'd ever been, he could not disguise his concern for my welfare. I sat down on his couch, completely overwhelmed. The Yiddish expression of my father played loudly in my head: *Ich hub niescht kain koach*, "I have no more strength." I found myself in a place I had never been before. If you ask anyone I know to describe me, you would hear something along the lines of, "Naomi's the happiest person I've ever met." Being happy and full of positive energy is my signature characteristic. And although joy and exuberance is the true and natural state of my soul, I had been using food to mask an underlying depression of never feeling worthy or good enough. Two words I had never previously identified with—*depression* and *medication*—were brought to light.

Depression? I am not depressed! I have the ability to sprint forward, be successful in many professional worlds, have a beautiful family and home. Medication? I am not crazy and I am not sick. Why would I need medication? I've been able to handle life this far with never relying on pharmaceuticals as a source of stability. Why would I start now? I kept trying to believe there were no cracks in my emotional foundation. But the truth was that my binge eating was a behavior that was directly connected to masking an underlying depression.

When your emotional state does not match your external life, there may be a problem. I found myself realizing that additional support could be a really good idea. Different types of support vary for each person. At that moment, for me, I did consider taking medication for a brief period of time, but as it turned out that particular additional support was not for me.

Contrary to some ignorant, outdated stigmas, taking medication does *not* mean that you are weak, or that you just need to buck up and try harder. Believe me, I denied myself many things that I needed over the years, and it did me a lot more harm than good. If medication is working for you, then I applaud you for getting out there, finding what you need, and being smart enough to give it to yourself. Bravo! Nobody, and I mean *nobody*, can tell you what you feel, or what to do with your body. Each individual needs to decide for themselves. There is no universal right or wrong.

I had hit rock bottom and felt vulnerable and helpless. And even though I understood where, when, and how binge and sprint began, my bingeing and sprinting were still ever present. I knew the underlying Dark Voice had kept it alive all these years, and the effect my dad's screaming had on me, but I also realized how his own Dark Voice drove him to do it. As it turns out, even when we are enlightened as to how our underlying psyche works, our lives don't magically turn around. What I thought was the end of my turmoil was just the beginning of unraveling all I had learned. I always thought that recovery meant that *poof,* you arrived and now you were ironclad against any and all angst. Not so much. It was like being born anew, but with all the baggage from my past life.

I still had my bingeing habits, low self-worth, and felt the need to prove myself, all without an understanding of where to turn next. All of the paths appeared to be a dead end. It was time for a new game plan. Although I didn't have all the inner strength I needed at that point to see me through just yet, I needed to start with what I had. My strongest allies were those living with me under my roof: my family.

I leaned on my family as a massive source of external support because recovery is not done in isolation. Everything in life takes a village, and recovery is certainly not any different. Wisdom comes from those who are our external supports as well; they don't have to be related to you. We all have a community of co-workers, friends, religious congregations, mentors, and countless others.

During the writing of this book, Laura McDonald, MS, LMHC—Dr. Sacker's professional associate and clinical director— suggested that I pose the following questions to my husband and children during my ongoing recovery. Our hope is that you may be able to ask these same questions to your loved ones, no matter where you are on the journey, and gain knowledge from the answers. I certainly have.

ALEX

When did you know there was an issue?

I never thought there was an "issue." Rather, I thought Naomi was going through the same weight cycling that I did. I did not recognize her gain and loss of weight to be related to anything specifically unhealthy. I never paid attention to what she ate unless she mentioned to me that she felt heavy, and only then would I look because I wanted to help her tackle a problem. I never perceived Naomi to be obese, and I was always attracted to her, so her weight gain was not a problem that required my attention.

What did you observe when things started to change?

If what you mean is when did I start to observe her commitment to weight loss, I would say that nothing specifically stands out. Naomi gained and lost weight, as did I. The way she presents now about her eating habits isn't measurably different than the way she presented in the past when losing weight. The difference is an internal one for her, now between her ears. The noticeable difference in her actions, to me, encompass far more than what she eats and how often she exercises. In the past, they were her goals. Now they are byproducts of the way she lives her life. It's not a quantitative difference but a qualitative one.

What are examples of support that were effective?

I think actions speak louder than words. Giving a person positive verbal reinforcement is universally applauded, but I think it's a sorry replacement for action. Telling your spouse or partner that they look great is the cat's meow, but approaching every evening like it's your wedding night is the lion's roar. I can't think of anything more reaffirming and supportive of body image than chasing that body wildly and often. Other acts of support include refraining from complaints when she left for the gym, throwing out junk food or "fat clothes," investing in little things to motivate herself, from sneakers to countless water bottles, etc. All of the things that I did were guided by the simple principle that the best thing I could do was to avoid getting in her way.

What insights or perspectives have you gained?

1. It shouldn't be accepted as a normal state to perpetually fluctuate dramatically in weight. There's something behind it, and there has to be something perceived in front of it to stop the cycle.

This is a rare instance when you need to focus on what's behind you to be able to focus on what's ahead.

2. Having lost and gained weight my entire life, I can share from experience that I enjoy my life much more when I'm lean. The heat isn't as bad. Getting up is effortless. Exercising shows instant gains. Intimacy is different (it just is). These truths for me are the same truths for my wife, and they're very likely true in your relationship. My point: Be smart with the understanding that you have about what your spouse/partner is experiencing.

3. Do for others as you want done for yourself. Like money, weight can be acquired and lost. Don't be a jerk when you are where you want to be. It makes for a happy, lasting relationship, especially if the tables are turned.

CHILDREN

Did your mom's relationship with food affect your relationship with food?

Sammy: Growing up, my mother was very understanding with our food choices. We were encouraged to eat healthily but were allowed to inhale sugar or fat-infused products. I have a vague memory of shopping at Trader Joe's and then going for pizza and devouring two or three slices.

Serena: We grew up in a house where we ate whatever our parents ate. Not only was my mom's healthier outlook on food better for her, but it was all the more beneficial for us. We now know the importance of food and the real role it plays. For example, after eating healthy for a couple of weeks I used to say, "Let's get ice cream, I deserve it!" And my mom said, "If you'd like to have some ice cream, that's wonderful! Go ahead and enjoy every bit of it! But what you *deserve* is a healthy body."

Sophia: Absolutely. How I view it, with every attempt that my mom made to have healthier eating habits, she brought healthier foods into the house and projected how she would like to eat onto everyone in the household. Growing up, I always had the option to eat an apple or grapes instead of a cookie and many times chose the healthier option because, honestly, I liked it better.

How do you think your mom changed the most?

Sammy: When I was a kid, I remember looking at other mothers and then looking at my own and thinking, "One of these things is not like the other." My mother watched what she put in her mouth and encouraged us to follow suit. As she went through some tough times and turned back to the food, I watched and wondered. Then, coming home one summer, I found she was hitting the weights, eating healthy meals, and generally kicking it in the health department, inspiring me to start off my own journey to become a happier and healthier person.

Serena: My mom changed in her eating habits but mindset as well. She now knows that one way of eating isn't for everyone, but binge eating definitely isn't for anyone! Once you change one aspect of your life, all else follows. By changing her outlook on food, her perception of leading a healthy lifestyle altogether shifted, making her calmer and more consistent.

Sophia: I think that my mom became more comfortable with the way she views everything and with trusting that she can make the right decisions for herself.

What have you learned from your mom's experience?

Sammy: Struggle stinks, but through it, one becomes awe-inspiring.

Serena: My mom always taught us that we can put our mind to whatever we set out to do, but this is just another example of her proving it to us! Having such a strong-willed mom sets the example for how I want to lead my life. Watching her overcome so much, including eating habits, and seeing where she is now is a true inspiration.

Sophia: I've learned that everything in my life was put there for a reason, whether it was for the better or to make me stronger.

How do you feel about her sharing her story to help others?

Sammy: Proud. My mother always taught us that the best way to live was to help and motivate others as well as yourself. I think it's incredible that she is embodying that message, and I'm proud that I can help be a part of the process.

Serena: I think it shows the essence of who my mom is. Just like she wants to instill in her kids the best way to live life, she wants to teach others how to be one step closer to their goals. I love that my mom is sharing this because it's a vulnerable subject that not many would open up to, but my mom's always been a leader. I hope everyone learns as much from my mom's story as I did.

Sophia: I feel really proud. I'm proud of her and the strength she has to be able to write out her challenges throughout her whole life. I definitely think it's scary to share your life with the whole world, but the amount of lives we hope to touch definitely outweighs the fear.

Although I gained so much from my external supports, I knew I would never become the person I was meant to be without taking full responsibility and doing my own inner work. I had no choice but to finally surrender and turn within, no matter the level of difficulty and excruciating pain it would cause. I'm a firm believer in the old saying that G-d will never send you a challenge that you can't handle because you already have everything you need inside you to get it done. I learned countless lessons over countless years, and I received the highest of professional advice and family support. The time had come to do the inner work and to apply all of it. To be brave enough to let go of the old, damaging coping mechanisms and create new ones for the life I knew I deserved.

CHAPTER 14

Recovery: Relaxed with Food

I 'm spending my time in recovery taking all of the practical strategies I've learned about food and finally, steadfastly, consistently applying them to my life. Not in a sprint, but one at a time, over time. Please understand that these strategies didn't come together overnight, nor do I necessarily employ every tool all at once. After years of collecting strategies through trial and error, I sample each one as I need it and slowly build them into my repertoire. Implementing some of them is beginning to become automatic, and I think that's the realistic goal here: *To work toward figuring out a way where you can be mindful of food and tame it so that you become the master. And if it ever threatens to get out of hand again, you have an arsenal of tested, proven, and effective strategies to put it back in its place.* Here's the work I'm doing that I know will get me there.

INNER WORK

My turning point continues to evolve through taking a series of short pauses, focusing on myself, seeing that the world did not blow up as a result, and then feeling safe enough to implement the following into my daily life.

1. **Self-care:** Being kind and patient with myself, and indulging in activities that make me feel cared for, worthy, and beautiful without worrying that I should be doing something else more productive. Some examples of my personal favorites are getting together with friends, saying "Yes" to spur-of-the-moment adventures, mani-pedis, and long, lazy afternoons with my family.

2. **Self-awareness:** Processing through core issues that are painful, yet leave me powerfully in control of my choices.

3. **Self-motivation/inspiration:** Choosing consistent exercise as part of my routine to heal myself physically, and learning to eat as a mechanism to fuel my body completely. My personal trainer, Debbie, has taught me to understand that we will all fall off the horse now and again, and to just get back on ASAP. Not tomorrow, not next week, next month, or next year. Now.

4. **Self-talk:** Selecting words that are positive, which gives me courage, confidence, and the power to move forward along a beneficial path.

CHANGE THE INTERPRETATION

As a speech and language pathologist, I have a passion for words, their meaning, and the value they hold. That "just right" word has the power to hit the soul in such a way that it can literally rock your world. Aside from the Bible, my very favorite book on earth is the *Merriam-Webster's Collegiate Dictionary* . . . for real. So when it came to surrendering the "Dark Voice" and transitioning over to the "Recovery Voice," I was ready for the challenge . . . but not on myself at first. So I began experimenting with the power of words during my speech sessions with my students at school. I would have them choose folders at the start of the semester with positive affirmations, such as "I choose joy," "I'm a goal digger," or "I've got this," which they would have to read upon entering the speech room. They would then find their picture and pin it up on the board. While focusing on their image, they say, "I can be anything, I can do anything, I can have anything. I am a winner!" After witnessing time and again the determination and confidence this gave them led me to believe that it would work for me too. I began to change the statements of the Dark Voice to statements of my Recovery Voice, and it worked. But first, I needed to kill the Dark Voice. Here's how it went down.

I was listening to an audio meditation where the instructor said to use visualization. *What is the feeling inside of you? What color is it? What shape? Where is it located in your body?* I figured if this worked for feelings, I could sniff out the Dark Voice the same way. I waited until I was going through a particularly difficult time and the Dark Voice came out in full force. I closed my eyes, expecting to see nothing, and then asked myself those same questions I had heard on the meditation audio. But then something unexpected happened. As soon as I closed my eyes, I saw myself in my mind's eye carrying a wooden baseball bat while ascending the stairs to an attic. The staircase was winding and narrow, and the steps creaked and threatened to crumble beneath each step. I was getting covered in cobwebs, but I kept following the Dark Voice as it got louder and louder. *You don't deserve it. You are not worthy. You eat that, you don't get to look like you want. Work is for you and don't concern yourself with anything else* . . . And then I saw it. The Dark Voice was on the floor under a small round window with spokes running through it. The cobwebs running from the eave above the window to the floor nearly blocked it from view.

It was a tape recorder.

Dear reader, I swear the Dark Voice in my head that controlled me for four decades was a freaking 1970s tape recorder like the one Mimi and I used to play Crosby, Stills, Nash & Young, Carol King, and Barry Manilow on in our room. It was an old, forgotten, dumb, harmless tape recorder.

Someone just forgot to press the Stop button.

I stood there knowing that what I should do next was to repeatedly smash that sucker to smithereens with my wooden baseball bat until it was completely unrecognizable, but I couldn't do it. To watch me in that moment was akin to watching a horror movie when you're shouting at the person on the screen to hurry and pick up the knife before the villain gets them, but the victim just stands there completely immobile.

I felt bad about destroying the Dark Voice. Because the Dark Voice that was in my head was the very same voice that was in my father's head. It was part of me, and it was part of my father. And I realized that my father and I had been through so much together.

What heavy load are you carrying that has become part of you? I know, it makes you want to cry just thinking of it. But you don't have to carry it anymore, and neither should you have to. You can only listen to the Dark Voice or your Recovery Voice, not both. You have to choose. And we both know you deserve the light over the darkness every day of the week. You can begin to take steps to stop the cycle you've been operating under with food and silence your Dark Voice right now. And you don't have to be cruel and take a bat to it either. You can simply put it on the couch and tuck it in under a blanket, or send it off soaring up to the heavens with a balloon attached. And if your Dark Voice is alive and well in a living, breathing person, there are different ways to put that to bed as well, one of which will be right for you. As for me, I took a deep breath, said goodbye, thanked the Universe for the lessons and the growth, bent down, and gently pressed the Stop button.

Here are a few examples of my recovery language that have replaced the Dark Voice. My personal Recovery Voice is G-d based, as that's what speaks to me. Although my messages may not be universal, I put them here in full disclosure so that I can convey to you the authenticity and integrity of my heartfelt messages. Please feel free to use my examples, or replace G-d with *Universe, Source Power, Source Energy, Higher Power, Jesus, Allah,* or whatever you connect with, or create your own.

Dark Voice: You don't deserve that!
Recovery Voice: I am a child of G-d. I deserve to be happy.

Dark Voice: You eat whatever is most convenient!
Recovery Voice: My body houses my holy soul. I treat it as the temple it is.

Dark Voice: How selfish! How can you take time for yourself when you have others to care for?
Recovery Voice: The more beautifully I care for myself, the more beautifully I serve others.

Dark Voice: Only work is for you!
Recovery Voice: It's good and healthy to make time for rest when I need it.

Dark Voice: You are not worthy!
Recovery Voice: I prove my worth time and time again to myself by emerging even stronger from challenges and helping others do the same.

Dark Voice: Shove this in your face to make you feel better!
Recovery Voice: There is no food that exists on this earth that will ever make me feel better. I feed my soul with light, positivity, empathy, and gratitude.

Dark Voice: Use this food to steady yourself, and move on! Hurry!
Recovery Voice: I am brave and already have everything inside of me I need to face whatever comes my way.

Dark Voice: Who do you think you are? Get moving!
Recovery Voice: My job is in the being of now, and I take my cues for what to do next from my connection to my higher power.

Dark Voice: You need this food to stop the pain! Eat it!
Recovery Voice: G-d helps me with all I need. I take his hand and walk under the protection of his wing.

Dark Voice: You are not as special as she is.
Recovery Voice: I have been gifted talents, insights, and characteristics that nobody else in the world has.

Dark Voice: Self-care was not made for you to indulge in.
Recovery Voice: G-d put me on this earth to freely enjoy all that it has to offer.

Implementing these affirmations is helping me to diminish the strength and power of the Dark Voice over me. Now with my Recovery Voice, I'm learning how to ask for help, and my intense need to listen to the negative voices in my head is waning. You can use a friend as an accountability partner instead or apply a different strategy until you find what works for you.

SET YOURSELF FREE

How you speak to yourself determines your destiny. If we use words that hurt us, we will stay in our dysfunction. But using language that is nurturing and uplifting helps us on the road to recovery and freedom.

How did I begin to find this freedom? I had to revisit my memories as a child. I was eye to eye with the eight-year-old me who started binge eating over forty years prior. I'm learning to accept that I could no longer live in the past. I am also in the process of forgiving the ones who have hurt me with their words and actions. Not like, "I forgive you and give you permission to do it to me again." But more like, "I understand that if you knew better, you would do better. I believe that you were doing the best you could with what you had. I take full responsibility for the part I played in our interactions, and I now set both of us free from blame." I wish the person well and to walk with G-d.

You have no idea the freedom I'm feeling with every step of progress I'm taking toward no longer dragging around my past in my present and projecting it into my future. The person who ran themselves into the ground in their business no longer exists. Instead of building from a place of fear, I'm now building from a place of love, excitement, gratitude, and joy, and it makes me so happy as the effects trickle down to everyone else in my business in such a positive way. Everything is changing. I reach out more freely to friends. My speech lessons have taken on a new, deeper meaning. I'm actually exploring, tasting, and enjoying new foods—something that I never did as I was always either bingeing or restricting. You will set yourself free when you realize that your worth is not determined by your jean size. It's the act of coming out the other side of each and every small battle that makes you feel worthy, and you have the power right now to do just that. Decide that your bingeing days are *over* right now. You will be amazed and delighted at the unencumbered feeling that awaits you.

ENLIGHTENMENT

There is a quote by one of my favorite Jewish philosophers, Rav Kook that I first heard in synagogue one Rosh Hashana during Rabbi Alexrod's speech. In his book, *Orot HaTeshuva 15:10*, he talks about when G-d calls to Adam in Genesis after he eats from the tree of knowledge saying, "Where are you?" But in the original text in Hebrew, it says *Ayeka*, meaning, "Where is the man within you?" Rav Kook comments:

> "When we forget the individual essence of the soul . . . everything gets confused and full of doubt. This applies not just regarding the individual, but all of mankind in the aggregate. Their sin always stems from their forgetting who they are . . . Repentance involves a person's first returning to himself, to the root of his soul. Once he does that, he will immediately return to G-d."

Rav Kook's quote only further confirms for me that all of us already have inside of us everything that we need to achieve our wildest dreams and goals. You have the power within you to change. Believe you are strong enough, you are worthy, and that it's your time. Do not give up! Keep going and growing, and you will find that change will organically become part of you and what you do. And that is key because success happens when readiness meets opportunity. Take back your power, dear reader. You've got this!

LANGUAGE OF RECOVERY

And so, that's my story of how I got on the road to recovery to dump binge eating, regain my power, and find a joyful life where I live in a healthy body that I now know I deserve. It took me forty years to do it, and I had some pretty incredible professional help along the way, but the good news is that you can start today. We are in this together.

Below are the top thirty-six (twice *chai*, as eighteen is the Hebrew numerical value for "life") lessons from my journey. You have a very, very good shot at ditching your own version of binge, sprint, and the Dark Voice. If a hard case like me can be on my way, well . . . I truly believe there's hope for everyone.

Here's what I learned in all of my infinite binge and sprint wisdom:

1. Comparison is a killer. It will kill the real, authentic, original, unique you. Bury that bad boy before it buries you.

2. Stamina and Grit are two great friends to have. Keep them close as they will keep you going when nothing else is falling in place.

3. Positive body visualizations are incredibly helpful, especially when you're sitting at the dessert table.

4. Eat for yourself and not for others. They're not the ones who are going to have to zip up your work pants come Monday morning.

5. If you are powerless over food, admit it immediately. Do not pass Go without being honest. Then get the help you need. You deserve it.

6. Accountability to a friend or someone else that you can call when you're feeling low is an invaluable tool. Even if you have to pay them. Don't hesitate to call, I promise they want to save you from the cake you are about to shove in your face. And conversely, you may be saving them.

7. Step out in faith. Even if you're not there yet, believe and act "as if," and before you know it, you'll be on your way to becoming the real deal.

8. Do not practice self-deprivation with food to save money or for any other reason. You can eat a lot better than you realize within your budget. You just need to get a little creative. And if you're stuck on a limb, I have at least twenty-five tasty dinner recipes made from canned beans I'd be happy to share. Great protein.

9. Remember to grab hold of your version of G-d's hand. It's always there waiting for you, and better than any meal plan regimen I've ever tried.

10. Get down on your knees in gratitude for the challenges. The harder they make you fall, the higher you will rise from going through them.

11. You're just as good as anyone else. Nobody has magical powers, so don't sell yourself short.

12. You don't run the world. There's a bigger picture we don't understand. Just hold on and roll with the punches. You will come out the other side stronger and victorious.

13. It's often during our most challenging times that we give up on giving to ourselves exactly when we need it the most. This leads to lots of extra calories. Remember to count yourself among those you need to tend to.

14. You are worthy. The fact that G-d in His infinite wisdom

put you on this earth is proof enough of that. You can't find your worth out in the world; you have to find it from within because you're born with it. You can't make it happen or go out and get it because *you are it*. And once you get that straight in your head, all the avenues you once pursued to find your worth are no longer necessary because all of the things you were searching for find you.

15. Never give up, no matter how many times you fall, and always finish your race. You never know if this is the time that your battle with food will finally end for good.

16. Learn from your mistakes. Watch for the lessons in the fire, and forgive yourself no matter where you are on the journey.

17. Find the core wound. For me, it was the only way to begin to settle my battle with food.

18. You have nothing to prove to anyone. You are a child of G-d.

19. Apply the Surrender Method: Submission, Separation, Sweetness. Enough said.

20. You can assign any meaning you want to your experiences.

21. You can go through the same event in a completely different way for a better outcome. In the words of Shalamar, "The second time is so much better, baby."

22. You can have everything good at once in your life, and *fargin* (do not begrudge) yourself some well-deserved joy. You don't need to sacrifice a thing.

23. There is no way to fill a void except for getting the root of it and yanking that sucker out like a bad tooth.

24. While we need to take 100 percent responsibility for what

comes into our lives, understand that hurt people hurt people. It may be the case that it's not you, it's them. Like you, everyone is just dealing with their own stuff, and if you're in their life you may end up being collateral damage. Don't take it personally, and do whatever it takes to rise above or out of harm's way.

25. Try as you may, you can't make other people change or make them happy. It's not your job anyway, so you can just scratch that one off your list.

26. Be an active participant in your life. Don't allow old, mindless habits to lead you and decide the trajectory of your life. There's a new sheriff in town: you!

27. You have everything you need inside of you to take you to where you want to go and be the person you want to be. If you didn't, G-d would never have put the desire in you to go in that direction. Believe it, feel the emotions, and put the action behind it. You've got this.

28. You can elevate your soul by caring for and beautifying your body that houses it. It's an easy deduction from there that you have *carte blanche* permission from G-d Himself to go hog-wild with working out, preparing healthy food, getting a manicure, or whatever brings you that just right diva feeling that overpowers the urge to dig into a bag of Double Stuffed Oreos. Because you're just too fabulous for that. And in the journey to feed your soul, you become stronger, smarter, and less willing to give up your sanity, your beautiful life, or suffer any more.

29. Commit to recommit to your healthy lifestyle on the daily. Whether that means preparing your gym clothes the night before, making healthier recipes for your family, taking

a break from toxicity in your life, or putting your hard-earned money toward a trainer. And that does not always look divine but rather ordinary because we are living our lives day to day imperfectly. The objective? Never get to the depths of despair that you once fell into before.

30. Get out of your head and quiet all the confusing thoughts and food wars that come crashing into your brain at once. Leave the past behind you, connect with your body and your mind, and let them tell you what they want for lunch. In other words, shut the Dark Voice down.

31. Make a plan by visualizing yourself eating specific healthy foods and then eat them throughout the day. You run your day. Don't wait for the day to run you. What military in the history of war ever went into battle in hostile territory without a plan of action? Do you think they got to the battlefield and said, "Well, I guess we'll just wing it"? Yeah, the planning and food prep is a time suck, but *you are worth it!*

32. Just like the cycle of bingeing makes you feel awful so you binge again to feel better, eating healthy makes you feel good, which keeps you eating what serves you. This is the same for any issue, like shopping, gambling, or drinking.

33. Decide that there is no better time than now. Not tomorrow. Now. No next-weeking it.

34. Live in "Why not?" Why not get out of bed early and go to the gym? Yeah, you'll be miserable getting out from under the covers, but halfway to the gym, you'll be so glad you went. Five minutes of sticking with "why not?" could just be the commitment it takes to get you to that simple soul-loving place.

35. Be your own guardian angel who will save you from your own destruction. Be as stringent and strict for your good as the Dark Voice is for your demise. Because if you don't stay in the light, you'll end up in the dark.

36. There is no food that exists in this world where binge eating it will ever make you feel better. (But just in case I'm wrong and you do find it, please let all of us know. Thanks. A girl can dream, right?)

As I reflect on this entire process, I pray, dear reader, that the tools I have left you with will further assist you on whatever journey you are on. May the lessons contained in this book bless you with opportunities for change and success like they have blessed me.

Acknowledgements

T rue to form, I'm going to have to tell you the whole story of how this book came to life in order for you to fully grasp the depths of my gratitude for all of the people who did nothing short of reaching way down and lifting me throughout this journey.

It all started in a bikini on a lounge chair in Maui at my network marketing company's annual incentive trip for top-level consultant earners. Amy Powers, a Harvard lawyer, Columbia MBA, long-time friend, and sideline sister in my company, blessed me with a few lines from her new book *Network Marketing: No Degree Required* (Utah: Winsome Entertainment Group, 2021). By the time I had exhausted my litany of excuses as to why it wasn't the right time to birth the book inside me that was dying to come out, she had already connected me with my now Fairy G-d Mother, Kimberly O'Hara, book coach extraordinaire. Amy, it was *you* who set me on this journey! Thank you for ignoring my objections, seeing through my excuses, and believing in me. You are in my heart forever my friend.

Kimberly O'Hara from A Story Inside turned out to be not only the best book coach there is, but a best friend, mentor, confidant, shoulder to cry on, ear to *really* hear, and guardian angel who elevated me to the next level in fully understanding my journey and expressing it in written form beyond anything that I would have been able to envision for myself. It was as if she took a three-thousand-piece puzzle and created a symphony from a once-jumbled, haphazard, and seemingly disconnected pile of stories.

And it was because of Kim's connections that were gained through her hustle and moxie for the betterment of her clients, that I, a very not-famous first-time memoir writer, was introduced to, and subsequently signed, with a traditional publisher. Thank you Terri Leidich of WriteLife Publishing for believing in me and in the purpose of this book. I could not have asked for a better mentor to guide me in seeing the wonder and excitement throughout this arduous process. How you have coached me throughout this journey with your incredible confidence and knowledge of this entire industry that never fails to calm me and make me feel taken care of. You can't imagine the love, respect, and gratitude I have for you, not to mention how lucky I am to have found a friend in you. Thank you for understanding why this story needs to be out here in the world. Together we will benefit so many who are suffering in silent desperation.

Terri then brilliantly paired me with editor Andrea Vande Vorde, whose patience and extraordinary attention to detail in carefully readying this manuscript for market will never cease to amaze me. Thank you, Andrea, for treating this book as your personal painstaking labor of love over every theme clarified and honing my sometimes-too-harsh New York words to express my meaning while still reflecting my voice. Thank you for helping me expand my Jewish vernacular to be inclusive of every person from every walk of life. Thank you for the long conversations that served to tease out the last bits of unresolved issues. Know that the readers will benefit as a result of including these resolutions into the finished product with integrity.

And then Terri sent me yet another angel, copyeditor Allison Itterly. I can honestly say that before Allison, I considered myself a grammarian—but no longer! I was completely "schooled" by Allison's meticulous corrections of my manuscript's tenses, use of italics, and punctuation while smoothing out my fragments and wordiness. But most importantly, I thank Allison for molding my sentences so they could best express the love and care we wish to convey to the reader.

What made Andrea's and Allison's jobs so much easier was having the legendary celebrity psychiatrist of eating disorders, known within the industry as "The Wizard," and the man responsible for leading me out of a forty-year abyss of bingeing, Ira M. Sacker, MD, and his professional associate, clinical director, and editing superhero, Laura McDonald, MS, LMHC, review the manuscript with a fine-toothed comb. Together, they clarified terminology, and both introduced and fine-tuned ideas to make them even more appropriate and relatable for those suffering from binge eating. Their process gave me a better understanding not only of binge eating disorders at large, and how to communicate my message more effectively, but of how to truly be a servant leader and give unconditionally from your very being. They are both beyond a testament to the goodness that makes this world go round. It's not every day that one is lucky enough to find themselves with mentors and friends who come with the authority of being the best in the business and are willing to openly give to you and your pursuits. "Thank you" doesn't even begin to cut it.

My beautiful children—Sammy, Serena, and Sophia—I'm filled with gratitude for who you are. The maturity you have conducted yourselves with, the support you have bestowed upon me, the understanding you have shown, and the advice you have given throughout our journey in writing this book is beyond your years. I am truly blessed that you were sent to me. You inspire me each and every day. I love you more than you will ever know.

Mario Alexis Joseph, the love of my life. You are my reason, heart, universe, and soul. Because of your patience, wisdom, support, and guidance, I am who I am today. Thank you for jumping on this crazy, wild ride with me. I can't wait to spend the rest of our lives discovering where else it will take us.

And to G-d: You are the hand that steadies me and my fortitude when all of my worldly strength has left. I put in You all my faith, and know that I am forever protected beneath Your wing. I take hold of Your hand and walk together with You down all future paths.

About the Author

A confessed binge eater for most of her life, Naomi Joseph received a master of science in speech and language pathology at Teachers College, Columbia University, and ironically went on to have a twenty-three-year career treating children with feeding and swallowing disorders (dysphagia).

In May 2011, Naomi turned down a full scholarship for a PhD in pediatric dysphasia at Columbia University to grow as an independent consultant with a health and wellness network marketing company. As a thriving and seasoned entrepreneur, she continues to work tirelessly to grow her business by helping others find their best, healthiest lives and help others grow businesses of their own.

Naomi is overjoyed at being able to share her forty-year binge eating and recovery journey with whoever could benefit from her experience. Her goal in life is to touch as many souls as possible and give them all the healing her story, examples, and advice can provide.

Naomi has been married to her husband, Alex (Mario Alexis, yes, Jewish from Argentina), since 1992. They shared the bond of both having been the "chubby kid" on their first date, and reside on Long Island with their three children: twins Sammy and Serena, and Sophia.